THE HEALING POWER OF A SONG

Stories from the Life of a Volunteer

HENRY ANDREW

The Healing Power of a Song
Copyright © 2024 by Henry Andrew

All rights reserved. No part of this publication may be reproduced, distributed, or transmitted in any form or by any means, including photocopying, recording, or other electronic or mechanical methods, without the prior written permission of the author, except in the case of brief quotations embodied in critical reviews and certain other non-commercial uses permitted by copyright law.

Tellwell Talent
www.tellwell.ca

ISBN
978-1-998482-97-9 (Hardcover)
978-1-998482-95-5 (Paperback)
978-1-998482-98-6 (eBook)

TABLE OF CONTENTS

Dedication v
Acknowledgement vii
Praise For The Author ix
Introduction xi

Chapter 1	Oh, What A Night 1
Chapter 2	Premonitions Or Fate 7
Chapter 3	I Sure Glad Ya Not My Dahtor, Man! 9
Chapter 4	While My Guitar Gently Weeps 11
Chapter 5	Holding Hands 15
Chapter 6	Where No One Stands Alone 19
Chapter 7	What's For Dinner? 23
Chapter 8	Never Cash Out 27
Chapter 9	Gene Simmons – Last Kiss 31
Chapter 10	His Silence Spoke Volumes 35
Chapter 11	If My Monk Wanted To Dance 39
Chapter 12	You Are My Sunshine 43
Chapter 13	Pay Forward 47
Chapter 14	No Butts About It 51
Chapter 15	It's My Time To Go 55
Chapter 16	I Love Music 59
Chapter 17	Better When I'm Dancing 61
Chapter 18	Looking At His Watch Again 63
Chapter 19	Pray Harder 67
Chapter 20	Whatsa Matter You! 71
Chapter 21	Life On The Beach 75
Chapter 22	Saving A Life 79

Chapter 23	I Can't Believe You're Still Here	83
Chapter 24	She Remembered My Voice	87
Chapter 25	Miss Andrews	93
Chapter 26	Oliver And The Politician	97
Chapter 27	On The Road Again	101
Chapter 28	Workplace Charitable Campaign	107
Chapter 29	History Set To Music	111
Chapter 30	How Did She Know	115
Chapter 31	More Than A Century	119
Chapter 32	The Essay	123
Chapter 33	Kindred Spirits	125
Chapter 34	The Healing Power Of A Song	127

DEDICATION

In memory of my father Angelo
To my wife Carole-Anne
My sons Paul and Jean
Grandchildren Kayla and Lucas

ACKNOWLEDGEMENT

Thank you to all the hospital and senior residence staff members who work so tirelessly in providing the best care for their patients. Their love and compassion are always steadfast and even more evident during the peak of the Covid-19 pandemic.

Thank you to all those patients I have called "living history books," who have written their last chapter, and to those whose last chapter is yet to be written; I embrace you all with a great appreciation for your contributions to my generation, as well as to my children's and grandchildren's future.

I want to thank my generous bandmates John, Adèle and (posthumously) Richard for supporting my mission to improve the lives of those in need.

A special thank you to all my friends for their continued friendship, love and support.

PRAISE FOR THE AUTHOR

Recipient of the Governor General Sovereign's Medal for Volunteers 2018

"The Sovereign's Medal for Volunteer is awarded to Henri Arthur Lacroix in recognition of your volunteer contributions." Julie Payette, Governor General of Canada

"Neither the nature of the award ceremony - nor even the medal itself, can be a higher honor than the place he holds in the hearts of the countless hospital patients Henri has comforted with his music over so many years. The medal is a beautiful symbol of his devoted commitment to that volunteer work." Dwight Whalen, newspaper and magazine columnist, Niagara Falls, Ontario

"Allow me to offer you my sincere congratulations for being the volunteer of the year. This is a testimony that clearly expresses the importance of your community involvement. Time is the energy put at the service of your fellow citizens, resulting in exceptional work, which deserves you today, the respect, recognition and admiration of all." Barry Moore, Member of Parliament for Pontiac-Gatineau-Labelle 1992

INTRODUCTION

REWARDING AND LASTING LEGACY

My experiences as a volunteer in hospitals, senior residences, in church, and with charitable organizations began after watching a Public Broadcasting Service (PBS) special on Leo Buscaglia (also known as "Doctor Love"), an American author, motivational speaker and professor in the Department of Special Education at the University of Southern California. He emphasized the fact that we all have something to give to others. You have hands to hold someone else's hands, providing solace when it is needed most; you have ears to listen to their stories; you have eyes to share in the beauty of life. If you have a talent or ability in your field, if you can show genuine care, compassion and kindness toward all human beings, regardless of their background or beliefs, you have the making of a dedicated volunteer.

Recounting my stories, I realize that during my early teen years, I was being groomed by my own experiences of tragedy, loss, pain, suffering and loneliness. This laid the foundation for a better understanding of what volunteerism in hospitals and retirement centers entails.

As music is the universal language of mankind, I use it to fulfill my mission to take the recipients back with a song or a story, evoking positive emotions and memories of sights and sounds from a particular time in their lives. I am grateful to all those individuals for trusting and sharing their personal lives and stories with me.

Death is not the main theme of my stories but simply a part of it. I have enjoyed the wit and the uncensored revelations from some of the funniest seniors I have ever met, putting aside their state of being.

An unknown author wrote, "Before we die we plant a tree, have a child and write a book." I believe the best way for me to continue to serve humanity is to write a book sharing my experiences and stories of my life as a volunteer, hoping it may influence others to give their time and love, and leave a rewarding legacy. I hope my first literary endeavor will make my wife, sons, grandchildren, family and friends proud.

CHAPTER 1

OH, WHAT A NIGHT

On Sunday February 9th 1964, at 8 pm, I was working at a bowling alley as a pin boy when four mop-topped lads from Liverpool called The Beatles appeared on the Ed Sullivan Show on a small black and white television set sitting on a shelf above a pinball machine. I was thirteen years old and consumed by this energetic, charismatic group of four guys, three of whom were playing their guitars and singing. Oh, what a night it was! The enchantment of this group was the motivation that stirred in me the need to learn to play the guitar and perhaps one day try my hand at singing. Unfortunately, at that time I didn't have the means to acquire a guitar, so I would spend my free time in my local music store wishing that one day I could have a guitar of my own.

    Mister Rossi, the store owner, was a kind and generous man; he would let me stay in the store for as long as I wanted, looking at all the various makes of guitars and amplifiers. I was in awe to see the selection of instruments in his store which for me was like being in a candy store, and I wanted to buy them all. He knew my dream of one day owning a Gretch Country Gentleman guitar, identical to the one played by George Harrison, The Beatles' lead guitarist. I did some babysitting jobs to earn some extra money and with the money I earned setting bowling pins I was on my way to saving enough to buy my first affordable red electric Hofner guitar; the cost of a Gretch Country Gentleman guitar did not come close to what I had saved in my bank account.

I wanted to emulate George Harrison's guitar-playing but I also wanted a Beatles' mop-top hairdo. In 1965, a product called Dippity Do was a gel introduced into the market which was at that time used mainly by women. The gel added texture to your hair and was strong enough to last all day. I used it because of how it left my hair looking. With the length of hair I had back then I would wash it then apply the Dippity Do gel, and after it was dry, I would run a comb through it and my hair became fluffy. It was the closest look to The Beatles' haircut, and I couldn't get to school fast enough to show it off. But it was not to be. When I got to school, Sister Adrienne Marie – my eighth-grade teacher and school principal – took me aside before the start of class and with her soft voice said, "Go to the washroom, wet your hair, *comb it back and part it on the side."* You can say that I wasn't very happy with her as I took my silent tantrum to the boy's room. When we met up years later, I told her what she had done to me at school and of course she had forgotten but we both had a good laugh. Today, Sister Adrienne Marie is known as Sister Lucille, her name at birth. She is ninety-three years old, and I now play for her and the laity at the senior residence where she lives. I still tease her about my bad hair day.

It would take some time before I became financially solvent enough to walk into the music store and purchase a guitar. In one of the homes I babysat for, the wife's husband played the guitar and he had it hanging on his living room wall. Once I was alone and the child was in bed, I took the guitar down from the wall. For this small scrawny kid, this standard acoustic guitar was huge. Though I knew nothing about how to play it, I would get pleasure just running my thumb on the strings for hours believing I was playing a Beatles' tune. For some reason, I felt that it was part of me, that it belonged in my arms.

A kid from my school lived on my street and we were about the same age. He had an acoustic guitar that belong to his deceased father and he knew how to play some basic chords his father taught him. I enjoyed being with him, listening to him play and paying close attention to how his fingers were positioned to form these various simple major and minor chords. I would spend the entire afternoon with him as often as I could.

I once asked him if he would teach me to play a couple of chords, but he just ignored my request. I was so disappointed but, in a way, it was my first introduction to volunteering, through his unwillingness to share his time and talent with me and no doubt with others. He had no concept of sharing his gift, perhaps lost along the way by a broken branch in his family lineage. As fate would have it, I was fortunate to have a co-worker at the bowling alley, Mike who was a little older than I, had an old acoustic guitar. Knowing my interest in music, he offered to lend it to me on a permanent basis. Now I had a six-string guitar with the first E-string missing.

To start me off, Mike showed me how to position my fingers to form a D chord. I needed the missing E-string to completely form the D chord so I took a little of my savings and bought a brand-new set of guitar strings. Now I had another problem: how to tune the guitar. Here, Mike came to the rescue.

With an old guitar chord book left in Mike's guitar case, I would practice putting my fingers as shown in the book and as Mike had shown me, to get a tone. Once I had mastered a basic set of chords it was on to the next set. I took the guitar everywhere I went, trying to master that first set of chords. I would take it to bed, strumming softly under the covers so as not to wake my three younger brothers. I would even take it to the bathroom not wanting to waste a single minute of practice time which made some of my family members slightly annoyed with me.

I was not allowed to take the guitar to my summer job in an amusement park so the minute I got home, I would sit on the back steps of our house strumming the strings till two or three o'clock in the morning.

By the end of the summer, the calluses on the tips of my fingers were painful but I was determined to triumph over this instrument. With money already saved and added to my summer earnings along with a generous gift from a secret benefactor, it was off to Mister Rossi's Music store to purchase my first of five acoustic and three electric guitars over the years. For more than six decades since the first day I put my fingers on guitar strings, I'm still learning new chords, new songs, and sometimes bringing back to life old songs from another era for the enjoyment of those who remember the first time they heard them, where they were, and perhaps who they were with.

I always loved playing for people and dreamt of one day being on a concert stage, perhaps with one of the Beatles. I asked God to give me the chance to sing and play in front of twenty thousand people. And God said, "Okay twenty thousand people it is. But it will have to be for one to five at a time." With nearly four decades as a volunteer playing in the hospitals, senior residences and at times in the patient's home, I can perhaps say that I have exceeded playing and singing in front of 20,000 people. But God knew by playing for one to five people at a time He was giving me the opportunity to learn from the infinite wisdom of a past generation, on how to live a rich and full life.

Growing up and being the eldest child of the youngest child of thirteen children of the 1930s, I have always had a deep respect and love for my aunts and uncles. I loved hearing their stories about growing up during the Depression and living through the Second World and Korean Wars and of love found and lost. And soon, I began to develop this interest in other people's stories, from my friends' parents, aunts and uncles and even grandparents. This interaction with them made me realize I had an affinity with the elderly; there was a connection, which was reciprocated. It was also my first foray into entertaining seniors with songs from their era, and perhaps, it was also the inception of a future life as a volunteer.

During a lifetime people will enter your life right out of nowhere and some will leave your life much faster. Some people will change your life forever and some people will scar you for life. Over the many decades of volunteering, I have met some of the most fascinating individuals in my life. Through their trials and tribulations, they showed me how to live my life to the fullest and how to prepare myself for the final chapter of my existence on this earth. Recounting some of my stories has made me relive cherished moments of days gone by former times.

CHAPTER 2

PREMONITIONS OR FATE

I was unaware that in my teens experiencing death first-hand would be a prerequisite if I were to become a volunteer with the afflicted and the elderly. Death is not a subject that is part of a dinner table conversation with family or friends. I once witnessed a patient who was fighting with death to cheat or beat the Grim Reaper from severing the last ties between the soul and the body. It wasn't a pretty sight to behold as the patient turned their head from side to side, moaning "NO!" as only they could perhaps see the Angel of Death at their bedside. Yet, I also met a man who welcomed death, had made peace with it and who was ready to cross over.

Whether we like it or not, as we get older, we can't help but think of how or when we will leave this small blue planet and we are compelled to come to the realization that no one is immortal. Some of us believe we will join our loved ones who have left us much too soon. Others believe when it is over it is over, there is no afterlife and no light at the end of the tunnel. But I'm sure when death is waiting patiently for your last breath, we all want our children, a best friend or perhaps a religious leader by our side to comfort us during the nightfall of our life. But neither children, a close relative nor a best friend are a guarantee.

My experience through the decades has shown me that many of us may die alone, without any form of love or reassurance that everything will be fine. To tell us, perhaps with a soft tranquil voice to go and rest, that our work on earth is done.

Do we really know when our time is near? I believe we do but we tend to ignore the feelings and the signs while some embrace them.

A premonition is defined as having a strong feeling that something is about to happen, especially something unpleasant. On the eve of my aunt's passing at seventy-five, she had spent the day baking bread, pies and preparing meals for the week for my eighty-five-year-old uncle. She must have had a premonition that her time had come. According to my cousin, as told by her father, my aunt got out of bed, kissed her husband on the cheek, went to the couch, laid down, crossed her arms and handed over her final breath of life to her Creator.

An Oglala Lakota war leader named Crazy Horse was frequently attributed to the phrase, "It's a good day to die." For this warrior, it was an expression of willingness to give one's life for one's cause. The phrase had a different meaning one spring morning for a man in a residence I barely knew and played for on occasion, who got up, was dressed, had breakfast and asked to be wheeled in front of the large living room picture window. He was admiring the blue sky, the season's floral abundance, watching and listening to the cooing of a couple of morning doves perched on a branch of a small tree in front of him. He turned to the nurse who was with him and said, "It's a good day to die," then he lowered his head in peace. Did he have a premonition and were the doves a spiritual sign that it was time to go?

CHAPTER 3

I SURE GLAD YA NOT MY DAHTOR, MAN!

During the summer of 1969 I worked at a horror wax museum in an amusement park which sat along the beautiful shore of Lake Erie. It was a great job where people expected to be frightened and I wasn't about to disappoint them. One time, I entered Dracula's cage and stood still next to the casket when I heard my victims approaching. As they stood and stared at the exhibit and wondered if I was a wax figure or not, I would wait a few seconds and then make a slight move. I gave them exactly what they wanted and paid for – to be scared. Their reaction of fear was followed by laughter to reduce the level of terror they had just experienced. However, there was an incident when my amusement at someone's fear was replaced by guilt. A young lad of African descent decided to go into this dark cave-like venue by himself and why he came to that decision I will never know. As he made his way through the dark hallways, I could hear him screaming in horror and yelling "help," desperately trying to find a way out. I had never heard that curdling sound of fear again for the remainder of my time working at the museum. When he emerged from his nightmare, I can't begin to describe the look of fear on his face. I also noticed he had scraped his arm along the jagged edges of the walls, causing him to bleed. I was eighteen years old and I had no knowledge of how to provide first aid treatment to his wounds. I managed to stop the bleeding, I applied a sizeable amount of mercurochrome on the scrapes and with several bandages I mummified his arm. When he realized I knew nothing about applying first aid, he looked up at me with these big brown eyes and said, "I sure glad ya not my dahtor, man!" At that time, it was a very funny situation, but in hindsight, I could not imagine the fear this poor young lad had frantically trying to find his way out of the museum. With blackened walls, not knowing where the next hallway was, with only the scenes lit to guide his way, he probably thought he was going to die, alone, down in the dark bowels of the museum. The park was about to close and the bus that took him to the park was now heading back to Buffalo. Unfortunately, the bus, shortly after leaving the park, collided with another vehicle and there were a couple of fatalities on the bus. Was the young lad one of the fatalities on the bus or did he make it home that night? If so, did the fear of dying in the museum haunt and scar him for life? Did he have a premonition in those grim halls of the museum about the bus accident and his demise? Did he share with his family at the dinner table that night the event of the day? Share what was, for him, his near-death experience?

CHAPTER 4

WHILE MY GUITAR GENTLY WEEPS

The 1960s was a violent decade starting with the assassinations of President John F. Kennedy and Medgar Evers, the American civil rights activist, in 1963, Malcolm X in 1965, and Martin Luther King and Robert F. Kennedy in 1968. If that wasn't violent enough there were Charles Manson's 1969 murders of Leno and Rosemary LaBianca and the pregnant Sharon Tate, an American actress and model.

On the evening of July 18th, 1969 I was visited by a high school friend I hadn't seen in a while. She and her fiancé were in the amusement park and what a surprise it was when they came up to the entrance of the wax museum. After a warm and tender hug, like all high school friends who hadn't seen each other for some time, we started talking about those good old days. The school we attended, which had recently been levelled to make way for a new parking lot, left us with only memories of high school dances, dreams for the future, the end of our senior year, not knowing what life had in store for us, and our bond of friendship which has never faltered. I invited her to be my guest and go into the museum to see the show with her fiancé. I winked at her and told her to stay as long as they wanted. To my surprise, her fiancé suggested that I go with her and reminisce more about our high school years together. I could not believe that I was given a second chance to reveal my true feelings for her since the first time I saw her walking into our home classroom. I had an instant attraction to her but never had the nerve to tell her how I felt about her and for the second time my nerves failed me again and this time with a higher degree of regret. Walking through the museum we were having a great time not really paying any attention to the exhibits until we turned a corner and she saw the final scene before exiting the museum. It was the longest scene in the show which depicted a couple of graveyard robbers who had dug up a casket removing the jewelry from the corpse. She was holding my right arm as we made the turn and upon making eye contact with the robbers, she squeezed my arm firmly and there was such a fear on her face she quickly turned her head away from the scene. When we exited the museum, I'm sure her fiancé noticed that something was wrong with her. Before she left, she hugged me one last time and I told her we would see each other again soon. A couple of days later my sister told me to read the day's newspaper. What I saw on the front page was a story about an accident involving a car and a motorcycle with the picture of my high school friend above the article. She and her fiancé were on the motorcycle. The impact hurled them several feet above the ground into a ditch. For me, the decade ended with the violent death of my friend on the night she visited me at the museum. She was only nineteen years old. It was the first time, in my teenage years that I had to face the anguish of losing a dear friend. To this day I ask myself, did she know, did she have a premonition of her impending fate upon seeing those grave robbers? With more than fifty years since her passing I can still feel, every now and then, a pressure on my right arm. She didn't make it home that night and I did see her sooner than I would have liked, resting peacefully in her casket. I cried that night as I was trying to play George Harrison's song "While my Guitar Gently Weeps," but I couldn't get past the line in the lyrics about the love who is sleeping. I will never know if she had a sixth sense of her impending fate and her passing still bothers me to this day. For years I hid my feelings about facing her death and by doing so I felt as though I was betraying her memory, but no longer. There are times my guitar still softly weeps for her as I do every year when I visit her grave.

CHAPTER 5

HOLDING HANDS

Carmen's husband had passed a few years before and now in her late eighties, she was on the final journey of her life. She grew up on a farm, the eldest of eight siblings who had a dream of one day becoming a schoolteacher. Giving her a good education was the furthest thought from her parents' mind. The chores tasked to her in helping around the farm, with household duties and caring for younger siblings, were the bedrock of an education she would take with her through her whole adult life. By the time she was married in her early twenties, she was tempered by hard work. Her husband found employment outside the village as a forester and there were times he would be away for weeks from his family and he would send what he could of his earnings back home. To supplement the family income, Carmen did what she could by doing odd jobs from washing or sewing other people's clothes or watching over other children while their parents were at work. Through some of her most difficult times raising their two daughters she managed to help a child in need. Rejected by her parents who knew nothing about raising a child, their frail unwanted little girl required more love and affection and Carmen, who had plenty to give, took her in as her own. It wasn't uncommon in rural areas in the

1950s to take in a child who needed loving parents. Her two daughters, who were raised with the love of devoted parents, welcomed this little girl into their home and it wasn't too long before they considered her as their little sister.

At her side, lying in a hospital bed, Carmen was surrounded by her three daughters. With her eyes barely open and unable to speak she saw the nurse coming into her room and greeted her with a soft "bonjour" and a smile. The nurse checked her blood pressure and the cold stethoscope on her chest checked her heartbeat which was slowly beating down. As the nurse left the room, she looked at the daughters and they immediately knew that their mother did not have much time left. The dying woman heard whispering around her but she couldn't clearly make out what was said, but in her heart, she knew that her time was short and she showed no fear. A few moments later she regained a bit of energy, as is often the case in the final hours. It's a phenomenon known as the surge before death which can happen before a person's passing and their alertness may give families false hope that their loved ones will recover.

The daughters spoke to me of the sacrifices their mother made to ensure that they too found their place in this world as their grandparents did for their mother. One of the daughters asked if I could sing a French song that their father used to sing to their mother. The lyrics, loosely translated, are about not letting the chance of being loved pass you by, the heart is less burdened when you're in love. As I started the song, the daughters held hands around their mother's bed. Then the unexpected happened. Three nurses came into the room and joined the daughters, along with my wife, in holding hands. They all sang the chorus with me and you could see this smile upon their mother's face as she knew that it was time to let go.

Carmen died shrouded with the soft melody of a song she knew so well that her husband used to sing to her, and surrounded with the love of family that was handed down to her from generation to generation, and by dedicated health providers. Being in that room as a volunteer, I could see the importance of my presence. The song provided a source of joy, relief and decreased anxiety to the family members as their loved one quietly crossed over.

CHAPTER 6

WHERE NO ONE STANDS ALONE

It was on a Sunday afternoon in late September I was scheduled to play a senior residence. When I arrived, I made my way to the elevator up to the second floor. As I exited the elevator, the dining area was off to my left and in the doorway I noticed a woman talking on the phone, sobbing, and another younger woman was standing next to her. They were so engaged in the conversation they didn't notice my walking into the area with my guitar and songbook in hand. As I usually do, I used a three-tiered dining cart from the dining area for my large three ring songbook, which I place on the top of the cart and use the lower level to store my guitar case.

    I was just in the process of tuning the guitar as the woman finished her conversation then handed the phone over to the younger woman. When she turned around and noticed me, her demeanor changed completely. She smiled and said "Oh, music!" I told her I visit this residence once a month, at two pm, doing a different floor every month. She asked if I could go into her husband's room to play for him. I said it would be my pleasure. I also told her that I go from room to room starting at the far end of the hallway and that I would be in his room in about thirty to forty-five minutes. But something in the way she asked and the slight change of tone in her voice told me that she wanted me to go right away to his room. She said the entire family members were there with their father.

Following her to his room, she was saying how her husband loved music, especially country music, but I had a feeling that her husband was probably in the final hour of his life. As I walked into the room, I couldn't believe what I was seeing. Her husband had died that morning at ten o'clock and the family were still waiting for the doctor to confirm his passing more than four hours later. I have never experienced something like what I saw in that room. For the first time, I was looking at the face of death. Here was this gentleman who had a greyish complexion and his lips were blue and his stomach was slightly bloated. The veins on his face looked like cracks you would see on the face of an old antique porcelain doll. His mouth was open as were his eyes, looking up at the ceiling.

Now what am I to do? Do I tell them that I was unable to do what his wife asked of me, that I didn't have the fortitude to play or sing? Now I had to make a quick decision on whether I stay or leave. Looking at all the family members who stood there like statues and the expression of deep grief on their faces, may have been asking themselves, will he play or will he just turn around and leave the room? Unlike the young boy in the museum or the loss of my high school friend, I had to deal with death, and this time I was staring straight at it.

Without revealing my true feelings about what they were asking of me, I summoned enough courage to play for this man, but moreover, I had to decide what to play for him. Going through the pages of my songbook to find the appropriate song for the predicament I was in I decided to deviate from the country music he loved and played a gospel song. I felt that the song would reassure the family that their loved one was going to or had already arrived in a better place. I sang an Elvis gospel, "Where No One Stands Alone." Elvis won three Grammy awards, and all for his Gospel recordings. At the end of the song, with their tears still washing away the loss off their faces, I knew I had selected the right song. They all expressed their appreciation for what I had done not for only themselves, but for their father. I conveyed my deepest sympathy to the family and walked out of the room. The sight of that departed soul, as horrific as it may be for some, can also be seen as to what being at peace really looks like, and the freedom from pain and suffering.

CHAPTER 7

WHAT'S FOR DINNER?

As we grow older we all have our stories to tell of times past and we welcome those who are willing to listen to them. When I walk into a room I never really know what kind of stories to expect or what kind of new experience awaits me.

It's a sunny fall day, a woman of short stature with white hair which tells of a life well lived and wisdom earned, is pondering out her hospital window gazing at Mother Nature's tapestry of colors. She reminds me of my godmother and is deep in thought, perhaps going through her seasons of a life once filled with the love of her long-departed husband. Their loving union blessed them with their only child, a son. Perhaps she was thinking, as well, of her friends and the birth of their children, the times they shared during birthdays, Christmas holidays and picnics in the park. Her son, a successful lawyer, never missed dinner with his mother despite his heavy workload. I had seen him on several occasions and we had wonderful talks about his profession, my volunteer work and of course, his mother. With her eyesight and motor skills failing her, it was burdensome for her to feed herself. He knew that he had to care for her as she did from the day he was born. When I entered her room and after a few moments of small talk she would tell me, with this gleam in her eyes, that she expected her son any minute for dinner. Of course, he was there without fail and she welcomed him with a deep love and affection shrouded in a warm gentle embrace that can only come from a mom.

I will always remember one afternoon before I made my way to her room, I learned of her son's passing. He was in his late forties, dying of a massive heart attack. It wasn't a time for music but a moment to comfort her during her period of grief. I sat with her and listened to her speak, as tears filled her eyes, of the two greatest loves of her life, her son and husband. At one point, she became a bit angry and said, "Why doesn't God take me and not take those who are younger?"

It was dinner time and she knew her son wouldn't be walking into her room to hold her hand and share in a conversation while he fed her. A nurse came in with her supper, placed it on the table in front of her, wished her "bon appetite," and left. As a volunteer, I am not permitted to help a patient straighten up in bed or move the patient out of bed to a chair, let alone feed the patient dinner or lunch. Being short-staffed, the nurses would not be able to feed her in time and her meal would be cold. I could not stand by and let that happen despite hospital protocol.

She wanted to know "what's for supper?" Knowing full well that a typical hospital meal entails a selection of some kind of meat, or "freshly" made sandwich, hot or cold soup, pudding, hot or cold coffee and the main staple of any hospital lunch or dinner, the nauseating jiggling of green Jello, I decided to make her evening dinner a memorable one. I told her this evening's meal was provided by a renowned French chef from the Café Chez Henri, that I would be her waiter, and that "tonight's menu will surely titillate the palate.

Madam, tonight we are serving a top choice cut of filet mignon cooked to perfection, served with potato purée, topped with béarnaise sauce, seasonal vegetables and a slice of the finest French bread. For dessert, you will be having a generous slice of a Boston cream pie, topped with the finest whipped cream prepared in the kitchen of Café Chez Henri, and served with a hot cup of their finest green tea." Of course, she knew I was lying but it did put a smile on her face.

I started by cutting her meat in very small pieces, picking it up on a fork and feeding her. Naturally, we had a conversation about her son and how she misses him. I must have met with her approval for feeding her, something I have never done before simply by the sincere appreciation in her eyes and her gentle touch of thanks as she warmly cupped my hand to hers. After she ate but a small portion of her meal, for some reason she asked for "The Anniversary Song," a song by Al Jolson, usually played at a couple's milestone wedding anniversary. The song may have reminded her of happier times of dancing with her husband, with her son looking on as she turned – in her mind perhaps – the final page of her life. I wanted to be with her at dinner time for as long as she lived but unfortunately, she had been beckoned. She joined her husband and son a few hours later, on a day that looked a lot like the first time I met her.

CHAPTER 8

NEVER CASH OUT

I often think of those long evenings teaching myself how to play the guitar, sitting on the back steps of my house, sometimes under the bright light of a full moon and with crickets chirping. Apparently, crickets' chirping and high-frequency notes in the environment simultaneously arouse them which is an automatic response to sound vibration. As I was practicing chords and applying them to the latest three-chord songs of the day, I would look up at the sky and wonder if a star had my name on it. Would I ever become a Beatle-like figure in my own right? Holding onto my dream becoming reality, I kept practicing as many songs as I could and would hum along until I was able to find my voice hopefully in the same key. Crickets chirping to my chord playing is one thing, having the neighborhood dogs howling to my singing would be an embarrassment. I didn't want to take the chance and therefore I stuck to humming for a while. I didn't know it back then, but all these early songs I was learning were the beginning of a repertoire of tunes I would be playing for some people I grew up with and people I was to meet decades later in their sunset years.

I have learned through the years as a volunteer that when you think life is absent from the memory banks of a patient, you just don't give up.

In a hospital room, there were two men who were about the same age. One was quite lucid and responded well when I asked him what kind of music he would like to hear. The other gentleman had just arrived and his daughter was unpacking and hanging up his clothes and sorting out his personal belongings. She had a photograph of her late mother strategically placed on his night table so that her father would look at it while in bed before going to sleep. Her father was sitting quietly on the edge of his bed, his head bowed and his clasped hands between his legs. He didn't react at all to the song I played for his roommate. I got closer to him and I asked him what he would love to hear. His daughter signed that her father's mind was gone and that he was no longer cognitive. She went on to say that he barely said anything at all.

Music has always had a way of reaching people despite their physical or mental condition. Once again, I asked her father's roommate what else would he liked to hear. He gave me an idea of a song and I flipped through the pages in my binder for the lyrics, but within the first few seconds of playing the first chord of the song I had to stop. This "voiceless" gentleman with his head bowed asked for the song "Ring of Fire" by Johnny Cash. I looked at his daughter who was obviously taken by surprise and began to weep in total disbelief at her father's unexpected reaction. I played the song that may have brought him back to a joyful time in his life but it was also the most requested song I would play of his generation. He raised his head and his eyes looking at me and it was obvious that he knew the lyrics of the chorus verbatim which was evident by the slight movement of his lips. When the song was over he was still looking at me with those piercing blue eyes; he smiled and suddenly I had this feeling that came over me which radiated throughout my body. I had never felt anything like this before. His daughter walked around her father's bed and hugged him, gently kissing his cheeks saying "Papa, Papa." She looked over at me, her eyes still misty and with a soft sigh said, "Thank you!" Her father had never really left her, he was still with her. Music is truly the strongest power of healing.

CHAPTER 9

GENE SIMMONS – LAST KISS

Gene Simmons is a well-known American musician, singer, songwriter and television personality. He is also known by his stage name, "The Demon," as the bassist with the group Kiss, and for sticking his long tongue out while performing. I am not a huge fan of the group but I was of his television show, *Gene Simmons' Family Jewels*, featuring his son Nick, daughter Sophie, and his gorgeous wife Shannon Tweed, a Canadian model and actress.

On one of my visits at the hospital, I walked into a room shared by two women. Both women were in their eighties but their dispositions were worlds apart. One, who sat by the window, was the grandmotherly type; someone who could be your friend and a confidant, someone who was a storyteller and a source of wisdom, someone who loved beyond faults. I had been seeing and singing for her every week for a few months. The woman, whose bed was closest to the door was the opposite, with no qualms about what she was thinking. If she ever confessed what was really on her mind she would have to bring a lunch to the confessional. She had just arrived that day and it was her birthday. I welcomed her, wished her a very happy birthday and asked her what she would love to hear. I soon learned it wasn't a song she was after.

On many occasions, elderly women have offered me invitations to lay next to them in their bed. They all promised that they would be gentle and would not cause me any harm. But this birthday girl wanted a birthday kiss. I had made it a point, after having my butt pinched years before, to refrain from hugging and much less kissing female patients. I told the birthday girl that I couldn't honor her request because the other woman would be jealous. She didn't hesitate for a moment and indicated that it was the other woman's problem; she wanted a kiss and insisted on getting one; she wasn't about to take no for an answer. You see, sometimes my heart always seems to cloud my common sense and this time I was going to regret it for the rest of my life.

So, I capitulated! How could a small peck on the cheek hurt? It may just make her birthday a special one. So, with my guitar around my neck I got close to her bed and bent down to give her a small peck on the cheek. She had a sort of an evil look in her eyes and hindsight being 20-20 it could have been a sign that I should have backed away but it was too late. Like the wrestler, Dwayne "The Rock" Johnson, she immediately grabbed me by the neck in a sort of a chokehold. Unable to move because I was pinned against the bed guard and with my guitar pressing against my chess, she started French kissing me and moaning in total ecstasy. Her legs were going up and down along with her torso in a very erotic way. She had her teeth on her night table so her gums were wet and she had this massive tentacle coming out between her lips that was longer than Jean Simmons' tongue, going around my face. This woman was in a state of overwhelming emotion. If she had been anywhere else other than a hospital with someone else I'm sure, after their encounter, she would have had a cigarette or two afterwards.

At that time, there wasn't any Purell dispensers to disinfect my face and I couldn't get home fast enough to jump into the shower and wash my mouth out with the strongest Listerine to freshen my breath and kill any germs that may have taken up residence around my gums. I may have been able to remove her scent from my being but I can't remove the experience from my mind. This nonconsensual encounter has me reconsidering any consequences that may arise due to my heartfelt actions. I was taught a valuable lesson that day to just stick to the music, it is safer. Never again! That was the "Last Kiss!"

CHAPTER 10

HIS SILENCE SPOKE VOLUMES

I was sixteen years old when I was issued a learner's permit and within three months I was issued my official driver's license. I knew it was not a right but a privilege I was granted. It came with a great responsibility as well, not only to myself but more so for others when I purchased my first car and drove my friends back and forth to our summer jobs. Their lives were in my hands and I didn't take that responsibility lightly.

Every day we hear about deadly car accidents due to driving under the influence, drug use, falling asleep at the wheel, or texting and speeding. Yet some drivers, like teenagers, think that they're immortal, that they will live forever and never die.

One August summer night I was in a vehicle driven by a high school classmate, in his teens who thought he was immortal. I never knew what he was thinking behind the wheel racing at more than 90 miles per hour (144 km) on a two-lane road. The car was hovering and I feared for my life. I asked him to slow down but my request fell on deaf ears. He just turned his head and gave me this *don't worry* look. Seatbelts were not mandatory back then and what if he lost control of his vehicle? I must have had a guardian angel by my side for when I saw the flashing lights of a police cruiser that brought an end to my friend's reckless behavior, I was so thankful to the police officer and my guardian angel. Several years later this classmate was once again speeding, this time trying to evade police. He lost control of his vehicle and crashed into a brick wall. The entire front of the vehicle was pushed into the back seat. My classmate never had a chance and he had a closed casket because he was unrecognizable.

It wasn't the case for one teenage victim involved in an accident that spared his life but not his body.

I met this young victim as he laid in his hospital bed surrounded by photographs of family, friends and a beautiful young lady whom he loved very much and who in his mind, had made wedding plans. It was not to be. Andy was involved in a horrific car accident and became a sad and – according to his father – avoidable statistic. On a winter's night, his close friend apparently lost control of his vehicle on black ice, spun off the road heading for the river and continued to spin before slamming into a tree, sandwiching Andy's side of the car. The human body was not designed to absorb the force of this horrific motor vehicle accident which caused severe injuries to his internal organs and his spine. This handsome six-foot seventeen-year-old was left paralyzed from the neck down and unable to speak.

I had been seeing and playing for Andy for several months. Whenever I walked into his room I could sense that his broken body wanted to get up to greet me just by seeing his wonderful smile. I would take his lifeless hand in mine and shake hands like two good old friends would do.

Andy loved music. The radio next to his bed was always tuned in to his favorite station, which gave me a clue as to the kind of music he preferred. When I played a song he liked he would give his approval merely with a slight smirk and with this amazing gleam in his eyes. At one point, when I realized he just loved to listen to certain guitar riffs, I would put it in the song. Perhaps he himself, before the accident, was also in the process of learning to play the guitar and the riffs were part of the lesson. I generally avoid getting too close to people who are in a similar physical condition as Andy in the institutions I have been to. This is not only due to my past experience with a classmate who had a reckless love for speeding, which could have endangered my life, but also to shield myself from the heartbreak and pain that comes when young men like Andy pass away.

Before I knew it, I let my emotions I had hidden behind a wall surface, and through song lyrics, Andy and I were talking to each other, and he spoke volumes. This bond that I had with Andy could not be broken except by the inevitable.

In my heart, it was evident that we had become, over a short time, more than friends – we had become brothers. Andy was the exception to getting close to someone despite what I was about to face. His mother and father were able to see the effect I had on Andy's life through music and his reaction whenever they told him that I would be arriving soon.

On my last visit with him I promised Andy that I would spend an entire afternoon playing just for him – his own private concert. Before the scheduled day, Andy passed away and it brought back some feelings I had when I lost my friend years before in a motorcycle accident. I could have found myself in Andy's place – an avoidable statistic – that August night, due to the reckless behavior of a classmate behind the wheel of a car. When giving your time for the joy of others, one must expect the loss of someone who would become a friend. When my wife joined as a hospital volunteer, and knowing she is a very sensitive person, I told her that the number one rule as a volunteer is to never get involved personally. Well, I broke that rule repeatedly. I think often of Andy and the conversations we had through the songs we shared.

CHAPTER 11

IF MY MONK WANTED TO DANCE

He sat straight up in his chair, this mountain of a man of more than six feet tall, with his arms laying on the armrests starring out the large window in the sunroom, perhaps watching the traffic going by or the children playing in the park with their kites soaring above the blue sky. His face was strained with the passing of difficult years as he was looking at the world through his spectacles with lenses thick enough to be used as magnifying glasses. His hands were massive, which made me believe he was no stranger to working incessantly at his trade, perhaps as a farmer or logger or in a mill. After playing a few songs, I was concerned that he hadn't moved at all in his chair which made me wonder if he was still alive. So, I got a little closer, stared into his eyes and said hello then I checked to see if he was still breathing and I was relieved that he was.

His physical state reminded me of a time I walked into a hospital room with both patients I thought were sleeping. I would call out their names and I would usually get a response. One, whose bed was alongside the window, woke up and the other, by the door, was in a very deep sleep. I played a country rock song hoping to wake him up but to no avail. There was a curtain separating the two patients so I decided to pull it back. Perhaps the sun coming into the room would wake him up. I was in the process of pulling back the curtain when a nurse came in and told me, discreetly, that he was not sleeping, he had passed away. This deceased person did not look anything like the deceased person in the senior residence I played for a few years before. There were no signs on his face that would indicate any type of trauma prior to his death. Now the patient by the window was unaware that his roommate had died. He asked me to pull the curtain back so he could try waking his roommate up. What was I supposed to do or say to keep the information from him? I had to think fast. I told him that the curtain was stuck and that a technician would come to repair the sliding mechanism. The nurse concurred with my explanation, making it more convincing for him to accept my lie. I continued playing and told the gentleman that I would see him next week, hoping his roommate would be awake then to enjoy the music.

Now, the patient in the sunroom who was sitting straight up in his chair wasn't dead and he was still breathing. I played several songs from the First and Second World Wars, the late 1940s, and the 1950s, in the hope of getting some sort of reaction, but it was futile. Perhaps the man was deaf. The nurse confirmed that he was not. I learned that he lived in a small village where everybody knew each other and when they would have a celebration of some kind the only musical instruments, they would have at their disposal could consist of a couple of spoons, a washboard to keep the rhythm, and an empty jug for a bass tone playing traditional rural songs passed down by the locals. So, I took a chance and I played him one last French song, "Si Mon Moine Voulais Dancer," which literally translated as "If my Monk wanted to dance." The song is what is called in French, "une chanson à répondre," which is a response song designed in such a way that the listeners repeat, in chorus, certain lyrics of the song. There were many songs of this genre back then and there would always be one or two in the village who knew all the lyrics to the *chanson à répondre*. Once the song was over, this man who never gave any signs of life had a single tear rolling down his cheek. It is a given this song had a special meaning that touched the heart of this sphinx-like man in his chair. What brought on this emotion I will never know. But I know for sure that we could never deny or underestimate the influence and power of a song on a person's life.

CHAPTER 12

YOU ARE MY SUNSHINE

*"As a child, I'd be frightened at night,
she would stay and comfort me"*

I have been told many times by my wife that I have a knack of choosing songs for patients. Some may call it ESP (extrasensory perception), a premonition or a deep connection with someone I have never met before. Such was the case when I walked into a patient's room who had just arrived. There was something about this woman and I just couldn't put my finger on it. I felt I knew this person that we had met somewhere before. It was the way she looked at me and she gave me a smile that seemed to say, "It's been a while!"

She was a tall and svelte woman who exuded sophistication. So, I introduced myself and told her about my work at the hospital and the staff had named me the balladeer of the palliative care unit which she found amusing.

I asked her what she would like to hear. Like many people I have met, she too loved all kinds of music and anything I would play would be fine with her. I tried to find an era of music she may have been most familiar with.

I told her that my repertoire started in 1906 which is true, and added, "the year I was born," which is false. After just a few seconds, if I hear crickets about my year of birth, then I know that my attempt at humor failed. She looked at me wondering if I was serious. Then she realized that it was all in jest, gave me this wonderful smile and laughed. I suggested that if she preferred to hear hits by Frank Sinatra, Dean Martin or Louis Armstrong, I had a few in my repertoire. I went on to say if she wanted something from World War I and II or some 1950s Rock'n Roll, I could also oblige her. If she wanted a spiritual tune, I could render her a Gospel song. She said, "You decide."

    At that time, I didn't have an iPad with a program which allowed me to create folders on any artist and song for a quick look-up. I only had my large binder of lyric pages which held more than it should hold and if I flipped more than a few pages at once sometimes the rings would just pop open and my pages would be scattered all over the floor. So, to select a song, I had to go through page by page to find one she would enjoy. Within a few minutes of searching, I came upon a song I hadn't sang in a while: "You are My Sunshine" (released in 1939 by The Pine Ridge Boys for Bluebird Record). Of the hundred-plus songs in my inventory of tunes I could have chosen; I felt this one tune was what she would love to hear given her age. Perhaps I picked that song because of the brilliant sunlight on a clear blue sky just outside her window which made the selection appropriate. She sang the verses along with me but when she sang the chorus, I could see she was moved, that somehow, I had struck a chord with this song and her eyes were a bit misty. When I got to the chorus a second time, she turned around looking outside her window and she lowered her head still singing. I was wondering what she was thinking. After completing the song, she took a few moments to gain her composure and said that her brother used to sing that song to her every day. I couldn't begin to tell you how good I felt about choosing that song and her response. Then she took a breath and added, "We buried him this morning." I am unable to choose the correct lotto combination of numbers but when it comes to choosing a song . . .

There definitely was a connection with this woman as I suspected. But I truly believe it wasn't a connection I had with her but a connection I had with her brother who used me as a conduit to tell his loving sister she will always be his sunshine.

CHAPTER 13

PAY FORWARD

I have performed in many retirement centers during my many years of volunteering however I have never done anything in my hometown. I grew up, described by a friend, in a town full of railroad tracks, bridges and stop signs. In this small town, in the early 1960s, there was a Maple Leaf Milling Company, international nickel refinery plant (INCO), a shoe factory and many small businesses providing employment for a village of nearly twenty-thousand inhabitants. I still visit there one or two times a year to see childhood friends and family members still living in my quaint little community of Port Colborne in Southern Ontario.

On one trip, I decided to offer my musical services at the local hospital which brought back some very fond memories of my childhood. There was and still is today a marina in the back of the hospital where I would rent out a rowboat. I was about twelve years old and occasionally I would take one out, rowing myself and a friend onto Lake Erie. Looking back, it wasn't a wise thing to do. Without a life jacket on, we would row out too far and it was a challenge trying to make it back to shore. There was also a park where we had Sunday picnics with the immediate family and other times with aunts, uncles and cousins.

Walking through the front door of the hospital I couldn't help but to think of my high school friend who passed away there after her motorcycle accident. I made my way up to the second floor, introduced myself to the hospital staff and after providing them with documentation of my community involvement in my adopted city of Gatineau, Québec and the surrounding areas, I began doing the rounds. I was surprised to see people in some rooms I knew growing up during my primary school years. I remember them in blue jeans with cuffs, driving suped-up 1940s model cars with modified engines such as a Chevy and Ford pick-up trucks, some with a skull on the stick shift along with an eight-ball steering knob. Some would have a rosary and some would have a photograph of their girlfriend du jour with a pair of pink square fuzzy plush dice with dots hanging from the mirror. These tough guys had long sideburns and greased-back hairstyles which were shaped using a petroleum jelly that required perpetual combing and reshaping to maintain their frontal ducktail. They were stunned to see this once-snot-nosed kid in short trousers, a striped T-shirt, black and white Keds (Trademark) running shoes with white laces and a brush-cut they teased relentlessly, giving his time to entertain them.

I was hoping that the first room I walked into wasn't an indication of what my afternoon was going to be like. There were two men in the room and the one closest to the door had irked me. He had this look of contempt in his eyes and for the first time I felt an altercation was about to happen. Sharing the room with another patient, I controlled myself, ignored his presence and directed my attention to the other man who had a kinder and gentler demeanor. I spent a few minutes in conversation with him and I asked him how long he was expecting to be staying in the hospital. He had no idea but then he asked if I could play a special song for him. I said if I knew the song, it would be my pleasure to do it for him. He requested "Why Me Lord?" by Kris Kristofferson. Requesting this song may have been what he needed to find his way back to God. The arrogant patient was sitting up in his bed; a once-tough guy who was a bully in his day and probably still was, arms stretched out covered with tattoos (one of a heart with the word mother in the middle and another with a rope tied around an anchor). After the end of the song for his roommate he said in his belittling tone of voice, "I bet you get paid a lot of money doing this!" I replied, in a manner unbecoming for a person who holds a high regard and respect for everyone and said, "Listen, I don't get paid a cent for this so do you want to hear something or not?"

"Yea," he said!

I played "Don't Be Cruel," Elvis's 1956 number-one hit. In a way, I was sending him a response to his warm welcome when I walked into the room.

After completing the song, I followed it up with a Beatles' song, "With a Little Help from My Friends," and this former tough guy simply said, "Thank you."

I replied, "The way you can thank me is to be there for anyone who is in need for whatever reason and don't ask for anything in return." He just nodded his head as a positive response to my request.

I could not believe that his attitude had changed within a few minutes. I concluded that my message got through to him via lyrics of a gospel song, a song of a love that's true and one of friendship. Once again, the healing power of song prevailed. I shook his hand in amity, wished them both a speedy recovery and left the room feeling good that

I was able to turn a bully's anger around, helping him to reflect on his life which may lead him to positive changes in the future. I am also certain that one day he will help others in need. Was it fate that led me to his room?

CHAPTER 14

NO BUTTS ABOUT IT

I remember the times when as a young adult I would spend weekends at my friend's home where we would share some of the finest Italian table mains such as homemade red wines, prosciutto and olives. There would also be homemade pasta and a spaghetti sauce prepared by my friend's nonna (grandmother) who brought the secret sauce recipe from Italy that had been handed down from one generation to another. Of course, you cannot forget the garlic – a staple in Italian cooking. Sometimes his nonna would serve pasta with the finest pesto – a paste that traditionally consists of crushed garlic, pine nuts, extra-virgin olive oil and parmesan cheese that originated from Genoa, the capital city of Liguria, Italy. There was also some great Italian bread and I remember the Italians would take a piece of bread and dip it into their wine. There are times I would dip my piece of bread into my glass of wine as my friends – non-Italians – would look on bemusedly.

    At the dinner table, after partaking in the crafty decadence of good food and discussions on family unity, it was time to lay back and listen to his nonno (grandfather) and nonna's conversations of the life and friends they left behind in the old country. They spoke of their small vineyard of smooth-skinned deep red berry, fermented to produce their wine, and the fruit trees and vegetable garden around their modest brick and stone house. Then it was time for nonno to share a couple of his off-colored jokes that his moglie (wife) and his daughter were embarrassed to listen to again. As much as some women would lead us to believe they are scandalized by jokes and stories with sexual innuendos or actions, women do change with age.

Case in point! Many years ago, I learned quickly that when I enter a hospital room, I play with my back against the wall because of an incident involving a liberated senior who was probably one of those women who burned their bras in the sixties. She was very frisky and not afraid to express her intentions in detail that would make a clergyman blush. I'm sure that if she were to confess her intimate thoughts to her clergyman, he would have to bathe her in holy water in attempt to drive her nefarious thoughts from her being. In her room, she invited me to lay with her in her bed promising she wouldn't hurt me. I told her that if I did take her up on her offer my wife would be very jealous and I would be spending many nights on the couch. I thought a little levity would cool down her lust and perhaps she would take pity on me. She replied with a seductive smile and a gleam in her eyes, "She doesn't need to know. I won't tell her." She went on to say that I would not regret a single minute laying on her bosom and that I would never experience what she had to offer even with any younger women. She went on to say in detail what she would do to me and there was no doubt that this woman was well-seasoned in the art of erotica. Never have I had a woman talk to me in this fashion; it left me flushed with embarrassment and a little uneasy. I politely declined her invitation and thanked her for considering me as her potential stud muffin and proceeded to the next room.

The women in the next room were no stranger to me because of their long hospital stay. I stood just inside the doorway chatted with them for a bit and then began serenading the women. After the first song, I chatted a bit more with them about their favorite selection, artist, or their possible day of release from the hospital before beginning my next song. I had just started to play when the lascivious woman from the previous room had snuck in behind me and she grabbed my butt with one hand and pinched the other side with her other hand. She laughed aloud and her eyes gleamed in total ecstasy, perhaps in a second attempt to get me between the sheets. She was definitely suffering from intense sexual deprivation. This woman had no scruples and she didn't care that what she was doing or saying was morally wrong and she kept trying to grab my butt again and again until a nurse took her away. Was I taken by surprise? Of course, and I quickly learned from then on to sing with my back to the wall, no butts about it!

CHAPTER 15

IT'S MY TIME TO GO

**COURAGE AND STRENGTH IN THE
FACE OF PAIN AND GRIEF**

His wife had a large hospital room located in the palliative care unit at the south end of the hall on the fourth floor. Her walls were covered with photographs of family, friends and some of the places around the world she had visited with her husband. There were a few souvenirs on her dresser of the Eiffel Tower in Paris, the Vatican in Rome, and the Acropolis in Athens. Sadly, now they were only unrecognizable symbols. She was stricken with cancer and Alzheimer's and her husband would spend part of his afternoons and evenings with her as often as he could. He would put her hand in his and speak to her of all the places they had seen, of the new friends they had made and the events of the day. Married for more than sixty years, he had many stories to tell of the adventures in their lives through their travels to the many countries I could only dream of visiting.

There are twenty rooms on the floor and his wife was the last person I visited before leaving the hospital for the evening. I would play a couple of songs, then I would spend time in conversation with him. He was a dapper white-haired, towering, eighty-five-year-old, well versed in many subjects. Before too long we developed a friendship.

    On one November visit, he started telling me that he would eat a small portion of his meal and he was full. He added that his energy levels had decreased and he slept more. He had seen a physician who had ordered several tests and he was waiting for the results. As the weeks passed you could see he was rapidly losing weight. In March of the following year, on my last visit of the evening in his wife's room, she was alone which I found kind of strange. He would never have missed a visit with her and he and I always looked forward to our weekly chats. I made inquiries at the nurse's station if they had recently seen or heard from him. That's when I was told that he was in a room on the seventh floor. After completing my rounds on the fourth floor I made my way up to visit him and I was thinking back to our conversation we had about his health in November. He was happy to see me again and he revealed to me what I had suspected all along that he had been stricken with stomach cancer. On my last visit with him, it was evident that his skin had sagged on his face and the chemotherapy had caused some height reduction during his treatment so he was no longer this tall dapper of a man. He looked like he had also aged ten years and his white hair was nearly gone. Despite it all he was in good spirits.

    I did what anyone who visits someone in his state and asked him how he was feeling. His reply took me by surprise. He said "Everything has been settled. My house is sold, my will is updated and I planned for continuing special care for my wife and now I am ready to go."

    I told him that there was still one last thing he had to do. He looked at me wondering what I was referring to. I said,

"You know the courage that you have? You must leave some of that courage for me when I get to my end of life." He said, "Listen, it's my time to go! I must go! I have had a very good life with my loving wife. I leave with wonderful memories and most of all I leave with no regrets."

In all the years, I've been visiting patients in the hospital, I've met several people who have passed away and I never met anyone who faced death the way he did, prepared and at peace.

This gentleman was not afraid of dying, perhaps due to his strong belief in God and the afterlife, something he spoke of often. He fought his illness with great courage. He taught me how to live my life and prepare myself to shuffle off this mortal coil. I guess in a way he did leave me the courage I had asked for by the way he accepted his final days on earth. I was blessed to have had the opportunity of meeting someone like him, for now I don't fear death nor do I want to see it any time soon. He crossed over peacefully in his sleep several days later. A couple of decades have passed since then and I continued to visit his wife until the day she went to join him.

CHAPTER 16

I LOVE MUSIC

Offering my time with seniors in institutions isn't always about the ailing and the dying. Through the years, I have met some hilarious, memorable seniors. A woman, named Mimi, who had been in hospital for some time and was waiting for her family to find her a senior care center had her daughter bake two guitar-shaped sponge cakes for my birthday. They were covered with a sweet white frosting and a dark chocolate contour. The border was covered with multicolored smarties to embellish the cake, a thin layer of yellow cream for the strings, plus two quarter-notes next to my name. One of the cakes I was to take home and the other was to be shared with those who were assembled in the kitchen for the musical recital. Mimi was the first and the only one who celebrated my birthday with a cake, party hats and blowers in the hospital and I was deeply moved by her kindness and generosity. The smiles on the patients and staff's faces were also filled with gratitude. It was a great and noisy time for all because of being on an extreme sugar high. That was one sweet cake! I knew I had gained a couple of pounds because when I got on the scale it didn't give me any numbers it simply said, "Get off, you're hurting me!"

In the early years, I would play for those who were bedridden first and afterwards nurses and attendants would take the time – which is no longer the case today due to staff shortages – to bring patients who could leave their rooms to the kitchen, where they were treated to a mini concert. The tables were set up in quadrilaterals and I would be surrounded by between ten to fifteen patients. There were two entrances into the kitchen area – one to my left and the other entrance ahead of me, facing the nurses' station. On this birthday evening, the party was about to get wild. There wouldn't be a woman jumping out of a cake as an added surprise for my birthday, but for some women it would be something close to an evening at a male strip club. A gentleman came into the kitchen from my left side shuffling his feet saying in his raspy voice "I love music, I love music."

Mimi was sitting to my left side and as the man shambled his way in my direction, I invited him to sit next to me on my right. It became obvious as to why he was walking the way he did; he had a problem with his nappy – he was losing it. A nurse who happened to be in the kitchen, realized his dilemma, made the necessary adjustment, and led him back to the chair next to me. I imagine that he was not quite comfortable with his nappy for he got up and started to shuffle his way to the nurses' station. His nappy needed a bit of adjustment again and the nurse did what she could to make him more comfortable and took him once again back to his seat. Three women sitting together were chuckling as they observed this poor man's malaise and the woman in the center said to the other two, "It's too bad that he didn't lose his nappy, it's been many years since I've seen one!" It is said that kids say the darnedest things. Perhaps this is added proof as we get older we go back to infancy.

CHAPTER 17

BETTER WHEN I'M DANCING

Many women would have been proud if they had a chance to meet this nonagenarian. She was expecting a visit from her son on the day I was in this ninety-year-old's hospital room. I had not yet started to play when her son walked into the room. Introductions were made and his mother began to tell her son of my visits with her every week and that she loved my music. He bared witness to the fact that his mom is indeed an avid fan of music, particularly rock'n roll. He remembers the house parties she hosted and that she was the main event, the life of any party and without a single drop of liquor in her system. She loved to sing and apparently, she had a wonderful set of pipes, but most of all she loved to dance. Affirmation to be true, her son would go on to say that once the music started it was difficult to get her off the dance floor despite several attempts by his late father to lead her away from the floor. She danced to Chubby Checkers' "The Twist," "The Bunny Hop," "The Mashed Potato," which was made famous by James Brown, and "The Wah Watusi" by The Orlons. Like most young women of the fifties, she had a huge crush on this shy boy from Tupelo, Mississippi, who didn't fit in very well at school, by the name of Elvis Presley. She had a hunka hunka of "Burning Love" for Elvis the Pelvis.

Only once in her life she saw him up close in concert and she had lost her voice due to her endless screaming. On one of my visits, I gave her an Elvis bobblehead as a gift which she adored and kept on her night table and kissed it goodnight, so she said, every night.

I was going through my list of Elvis songs I thought she would like to hear and she immediately said, "Blue Suede Shoes." I said, just to tease her, the one by Carl Perkins? I got a quick and loud "NO! The one by Elvis Presley." There isn't much of a difference between the two versions of the song but the faithful Elvis fan would not settle for any version than that of Elvis. I have played many of Elvis's songs for her but I don't know if her son's presence in the room made a difference but her reaction to the song "Blue Suede Shoes" took us both by surprise as I started, one, two . . . "It was one for the money," and off she went. She was fully dressed, no pajamas just yet, and lying in her bed the song put her in full gear. Her internal engine was accelerating. Her arms were waving to the rhythm of the music as would a maestro directing his orchestra. She was wiggling in her bed, her arms going from one side to another, so were her legs as well. It almost looked like she was possessed by a rock n' roll demon, or perhaps it was the spirit of Elvis himself that took control of her body. Whoever or whatever it was, in her mind she was partying again and felt like the life of the party. Her son pleaded with his ninety-year-old mother to relax, to calm down. She didn't want to hear it, "I love the music and I love to dance. So, let me be. I feel better when I'm dancing," she said. Her son, who was unquestionably embarrassed by his mother's performance, capitulated and let her be. When anyone who returns to their youthful years by a single song I perform, it is the motivation that sustains the continuance of the work I do. Hail hail rock n' roll!

CHAPTER 18

LOOKING AT HIS WATCH AGAIN

The thing I dread most when entering a hospital room is finding an empty bed without a bedspread, blanket, pillow and all personal items, celebration cards and photos of family members removed from a nightstand. I can't help but think the worst has happened. Of course, sometimes the patient left the hospital to move into a senior residence or was well enough to go home with a family member. It was not the case for a woman named Rose, whose body was consumed with cancer – something I had seen many times before.

    Rose and I began a relationship with a mutual interest, our love of music. We spoke about what music meant to both of us and the impact it had in our lives. Rose loved old and new country, folk, gospel songs and of course rock n' roll. She had her own song book with her favorite tunes in it and if there was a song I didn't know from her book, I would surf the internet for the music and the lyrics. I would then prepare the music and lyrics for my iPad files, and practice the song, at times for hours, to get it down pat in time for my next visit with Rose. With the number of rooms, I had to play for, I had to allow myself a time limit per room if I was going to see everyone before the end of visiting hours. With my left hand holding my guitar at the neck where the chords are played, I turned my watch on my wrist in a way that I could see the time. I would look, in a sneaky way, at my watch, not to make it obvious that my visit with her was nearly over. But I couldn't hide this from Rose and she would say, "There he goes, looking at his watch again." I know that her comment was just her kind way of saying that she didn't want me to leave, that she wanted me to stay a little longer. I must admit I would extend my time with Rose because I was told I was the only visitor she had, and she always looked forward to seeing me and spoke of me in a loving way.

Then the day I dreaded most happened. I entered her room and her bed was empty and there was not a single sign that she was ever there. I asked a nurse what happened to Rose and she told me that Rose was in a room at the end of the hall and it was just a matter of time before she passed. I was told that her blood pressure had decreased and her lungs were congested. She also had periods of shallow breathing that alternated with periods of deeper, rapid breathing. The nurse also said Rose would not know who I was and was not cognitive enough for her to respond to anything or anyone. I didn't accept that answer and proceeded to her room at the end of the hall. My heart was breaking to see that she was left alone in a dark room resting on an air mattress to give her comfort from the bed sores she had due to being confined to the bed for a long period of time. I opened the light just above her bed and I could see that her breathing was irregular and her face showed no signs of pain she may be having. I bent down and whispered in her ear who I was and that I was going to play a special song for her. I was sure that she heard me because hearing is thought to be the last sense to go in the dying process. I sang Elvis's "Can't Help Falling in Love with You." As I was playing the song I noticed, in

The Healing Power of a Song

the corner of my eye, the nurse, who came into the room probably wondering why I was there with Rose after she told me about her condition. At the end of the song, to my surprise, Rose's lips moved and though she was unable to produce a sound her lips clearly said, "It's beautiful." The nurse was overwhelmed and had a sudden strong emotion at the sight of what just happened and she could not imagine how a simple song could impact someone's life, especially at the end of that person's life. She thanked me for what I had done for Rose and she walked out of the room. I told Rose I would continue to play for her and promised that I would not be looking at my watch.

Rose passed away a few hours later that night. I attended Rose's church funeral service, which was attended by six people; the priest, two altar boys, myself and her two sons I never knew she had. Of course, there were never Happy Mother's Day, Christmas, or birthday cards, photos of family, nor even a small bouquet of flowers from her sons. I learned later that they were often intoxicated. Children can be a disappointment. I hope that my last few moments with Rose on earth comforted her, knowing she was surrounded with the sound of music she loved so much.

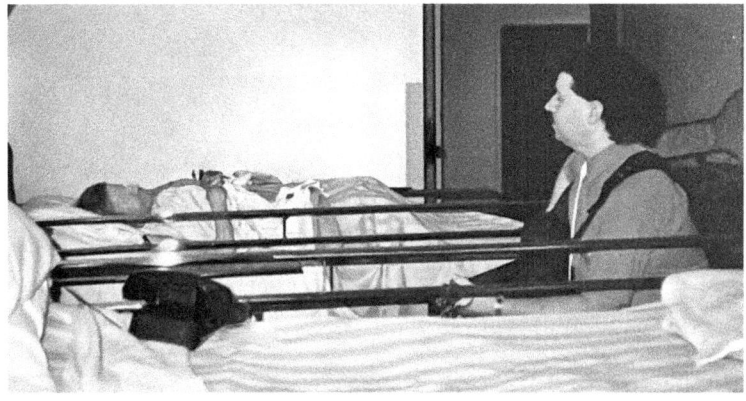

CHAPTER 19

PRAY HARDER

In January 1989, I had formed a band with Richard, a work colleague with a mission of raising money for nonprofit organizations. We needed to find other musicians who were willing to give their valuable time dedicated to the same cause. I was sixteen years old when I formed my first band with a childhood friend from primary school. John played the drums but in the early 1970s he moved away and although I tried to keep in contact with him, life always has a way of deviating from your initial plans thus delaying the reunion. It wasn't until 1979, when I decided to leave Port Colborne, Ontario and move to Gatineau, Québec that we would reunite. At that time, my life had taken a sharp turn. I had to deal with a religious issue and the consequences if I did not convert. I was also in the process of finally getting an identity; I was searching for my biological father, without any help from my biological mother. The pressure of both, along with the alienation of my siblings, was too much to handle. Therefore, I needed to move get my act together and settle into my new surroundings prior to finding John.

I was able to locate his home through my family members who knew his family. The time had come for me to make my way to his home, surprising him on his front door. It was a great reunion as we reminisced about our childhood and the first band we had together. The latter opened the door to tell him about my plan to start up another band, but this time with a mission to raise money for charitable organizations. I wasn't sure if he still played the drums. Knowing the kind of person he was back then, it didn't surprise me when he did not hesitate for a moment to count him in. So, he bought a new set of drums and became the third member of the group. Now we only needed to round out the group with a fourth and final member. This was the most difficult part of putting this group together. There were many musicians who passed the audition and joined the group, but they lacked the commitment to the mission and left after many weeks of rehearsing. It was very difficult not to succumb to the setbacks and just give this endeavor up, but I pushed forward. It was time to take a different approach in finding another musician. So, I decided to teach my former wife, Adèle, to play the electronic keyboard, and in a very short time she had mastered the instrument enough to be the heartbeat of the band. At last, the group was complete, with four members who were all on the same page, to help those in need. The band's motto was, "If there's a cause, we'll be there." It was important to do something for others – to give something back. God had given all of us a gift, why not share it with others?

    After a few weeks of rehearsals, it was time to go out, play, have a good time, and raise money for the many nonprofit organizations. Over the next five years the band played at many charity fundraisers. One gig we enjoyed playing for was at a dance raising funds to help send Canada's Sledge Hockey team to the Paralympic Games. In 1994, the team came home from Lillehammer, Norway, with a bronze medal.

"We've received numerous compliments on the quality of music and the cheerful ambience of the evening. Organizations such as ours need you to survive and grow" - Frank Arecchi, President, Sledge Hockey of Canada

One of the places we decided to perform was for a local hospital's palliative care unit. I knew someone who worked there and he introduced me to the activity director who was pleased about offering the band's services. I had learned from the activity director that they never had a rock n' roll band play for these patients before. They had other types of music and musicians, but they were low-key, like barbershop quartets or a string combo, but never a rock band. We found this to be true when, during our rehearsal, the nuns who were on the floor above us asked that we lower the sound. I firmly, but gently, decline their request because the health conditions or impairments of these wonderful people needed an afternoon of musical diversity-to Rock"n Roll. Ergo, I suggested to the activity director to tell the nuns to pray a little louder and I was sure God would hear them while He was dancing to our music.

Some of the patients who heard us rehearsing in the afternoon asked that they be washed, dressed and brought to the hall, whether in their wheelchairs, walkers or even in their beds. It was amazing to see these patients, some of whom had been institutionalized in this hospital for more than thirty years and never left their rooms for any other activity in the past. Some of the patients had suffered serious burns to their faces and body, some were severely paralyzed, some were suffering from a severe mental disability, and some from multiple sclerosis. In this large hall, the nurses and other staff members would wheel the patients in a circle to the sound of rock n' roll music.

Though our gig was not a fundraiser, just seeing the smiles on their faces was so rewarding and when we left the stage, we knew our music brought forth happiness and joy to all those in attendance. It was also a reminder that when you have your health, you have it all. The response was so great that we had to go back again and I may be wrong, but this time I could hear feet stomping on the ceiling from the nuns above. Perhaps it was not for the band to lower the volume but they were merely having a dance with God.

CHAPTER 20

WHATSA MATTER YOU!

I have spent most of my time with seniors through the years and on one occasion there was a young boy who became a fan and never missed one of my performances. His mother worked at a senior care center as the activity director and she had received feedback from the staff when I visited to play and sing for my uncle who was living there. The activity director asked if I would consider, if possible, performing once a month for the residents. Of course, I did for many years, even after my uncle had passed away. The staff would assemble the residents in the sunroom, joining my uncle and me in singing along, clapping hands or tapping their feet to some of the ballads I had in my repertoire that they knew as young adults. The staff also noticed how I interacted with seniors and the positive effects it had on their physical and mental state as well for the staff who would join in and sometimes, they would get the residents up on their feet to dance.

    The activity director had a young, handicapped son about the age of eight or nine years old, who had mastered with ease getting around in his wheelchair. His speech was limited but he knew how to get his message across. The residents would be sitting in a semi-circle and I sat on a chair in front of them with my large binder of songs on top of a small table and he was parked right in front of me. However, I would get up from my chair from time to time and go around to each resident and sometimes I would kneel in front of one, serenading them individually. As I was going from one resident to another, this young boy would be right behind me, maneuvering his vehicle with such precision that there were times I would refer to him as the Mario Andretti of the residence.

There was a particular song he loved to join in with. It is an Italian song that requires the participants to raise their arm, left or right and say "Hey!" after the lyric, "Whatsa matter you!" This young boy was so hooked on the song that I would have to play it more than once during my afternoon session. When he wanted me to play the song again, he would raise his tiny arm and say with all the strength his weak voice could muster "Hey!" I was told by my young agent what my next song would be.

There were times I would tease him and play something else. He knew if he persisted enough, I would capitulate and play it again for my biggest little fan. The residents found his persistence very amusing and probably believed he was part of the act and he was quite the entertainer in his own right. Following his request, he would wheel himself closer to me, raise his tiny little arms, and bend over, which meant he wanted to give me a hug. There can never be a more sincere, warm and loving hug than the one you get from a child like him.

On one of my Sunday afternoons, before getting out of the car, I remember having a feeling that something wasn't right; I was having some sort of premonition. As I walked into the front entrance, I would pass by the nurses' station making my way to the sunroom where I would see my biggest little fan waiting. Neither he nor his mother were there in the room and I wondered why. I knew he wasn't well and I never knew what illness he was stricken with but it had worsened and he was in intensive care at a children's hospital outside the city. No one outside the family was allowed in his room which saddened me. I wanted to visit him even if it was going to be for the last time.

A few days after his admittance to the Children's Medical Center, I received a phone call from his mother who wanted me to meet her at the children's hospital. Once I arrived, she took me to his room where I saw my biggest little fan connected to a ventilator, forcing air into his tiny lungs to help him breathe; to a heart rate monitor; and to an intravenous bag. His mother invited me to be with the family in his final hours, because she appreciated the joy, I had brought her son with his favorite song and that he was always looking forward to seeing me every month which for him didn't come fast enough. It wasn't easy trying to keep my emotions in check, but I bent over his little frail body, and putting his tiny hand in mine I whispered in his ear "What's a Matter You Hey!" That was the last time my devoted fan heard those lyrics.

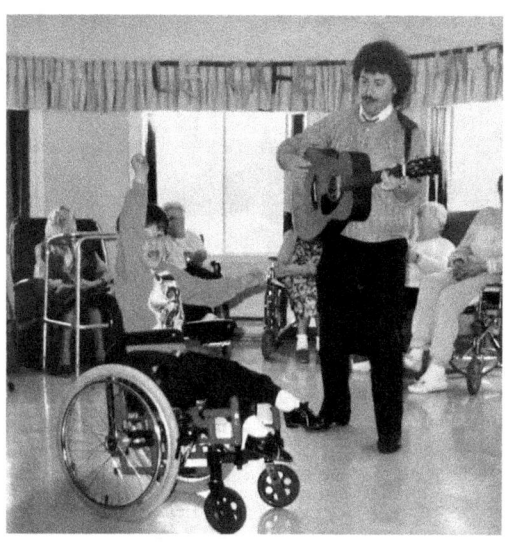

CHAPTER 21

LIFE ON THE BEACH

It was in the early '80s when I first met Arthur, living in a seniors' residence just outside of town. I visited him as often as I could because he was so unique from any seniors I have ever met. The residence where he lived was located on a hill overlooking this quiet picturesque country village where you could almost hear mice running across the field, and by late evening, a herd of deer would come out to feed at the edges of the pine trees. In the distance, you could see a winding river with a red covered bridge built in 1915. As a kid he would dive off this bridge, with his friends, regardless of the danger of the rocks and rapids below. He knew where to jump to avoid being taken away by the rapids or hit the rocks below the surface of the water. He was a scrawny, five-foot-tall man and the youth that once graced his face was replaced with one that looked like a recently plowed field. In his late eighties, Arthur was still clever and alert with a mind filled with stories of his past, a past that held a lot of heartaches. Despite it all he had a great sense of humor and he loved to make people laugh. He was delightful, and a fantastic storyteller who possessed an ability to hold anyone's attention with his quick wit. After spending a little time with him there was no doubt that his behavior was canny.

He spoke about the days as a campground park guard, on part of the land that was once owned by his father. Wanting to learn more about the history of the area, I took him out of the residence for a ride from the village to the provincial park. He led me to a side road in the woods and showed me the site of the house his father built in the mid-1800s which once stood overlooking a small lake. He spoke of the times he and his siblings used to fish and swim in that clear pristine lake. He knew visiting his once paternal home he hadn't been to in years, time would have erased any signs of lives that once dwelled there, now covered with brush and trees. Yet, taking a closer look, a square-shaped footing constructed from field stones was barely visible. To this day the lake still carries the family name and is now the campsite of the Beavers and Cub Scouts of Canada.

He lived there for a short time, with his first wife who gave birth to six children, four boys and two girls, before moving into the village. Sadly, his first wife died in 1925 at the age of twenty-five, and his four sons died prior to her death. In 1927, he married a woman he knew for some time and together with his two surviving daughters from his first marriage along with the six girls he had with his second wife, found himself as the only male in the house. This was perhaps the source of many of his stories and the birthplace of his sense of wittiness.

The story I recall most about his time as a campground park guard still puts a smile on my face since I didn't expect the story's ending. "I started my morning rounds," as he began his tale, "without a cloud in the clear blue sky and Mother Nature caressing my face with a warm breeze. The soft hoot of loons could be heard as an alarm clock's start to a new day and the campers filled the air with the aroma of coffee brewing and bacon and eggs frying in a pan."

Arthur continued to tell me that by mid-day the campers and tourists started to make their way to the beach, laying out their blankets and erecting their umbrellas. There was this aroma of coconut sun cream in the air on the bodies of the sun worshipers. The children, with their shovels and buckets, started building their sandcastles and forts. He went on to tell me how things have changed since the days he and his family spent time on the beach as a young man. He was appalled by the skimpy swimsuits women were wearing. In his day swimsuits were made of black-and-white striped taffeta with a sailor-style collar, black silk stockings, and black leather sandals. With a rather disdained look, he couldn't understand why women wore those bikinis, which left nothing to the imagination. In his day, society deemed women's bare ankles inappropriate and very risqué. He carried on by saying these bikini-clad women would be walking along the beach deliberately strutting their stuff to impress and arouse the males who were flexing their muscles despite several dead fish lining the shore of the park's pristine lake. Now I was curious to know why he would bring up the image of dead marine life in his story. What was the missing link? So, I had to asked him what significance dead fish along the shore had with his comment about women wearing bikinis. It is simple, he said, the fish would see these nearly naked women in their bikinis, their tails would get hard; unable to swim, the fish would die. This was just a great example of his humor and his life on the beach. At ninety-seven years old, he was still making me laugh.

CHAPTER 22

SAVING A LIFE

I can't begin to count the number of people I have met over the years who have come to the realization that they believe, because of their health issues, their quality of life had diminished to the point that it wasn't worth living anymore. These people who may have had once a lust for life had now resorted to an unhealthy morbid state of mind. This unwholesome gloomy interest in death was preoccupying their every waking hour. Some, who had their spouse, children, grandchildren and friends, had convinced themselves they had nothing to live for. They thought of ways to end their lives by cutting their wrist, accumulating medication for overdosing, or simply refusing to eat or drink. Some knew that people could survive up to three weeks after they stop eating and if the patient is severely dehydrated the body can only live three to five days. What courage or deep depression would it take to make it final, to resort to these types of deprivation and pain?

When I met Paul, he had been in the hospital for a couple of months following the amputation of his right leg. He was an active man with interests in winter and summer outdoor activities with family and childhood friends. He also had a love of music, especially from country artists from the 1950s and 1960s. When we first met, he exuded anger and bitterness, clearly yearning to be left alone. Undeterred, I told him of my weekly visits and mentioned the possibility of playing one of his favourite country songs during my next visit. He responded with a dismissive "Yea, right!" Determined to make a positive impact, in the next room, I deliberately played country tunes, hoping that the following week he would be more open to my presence. I wasn't mistaken.

    Paul wanted me to play a particular song he had in mind when I revisited him and to my surprise, he no longer had anger in his eyes and he also had considered three more songs he wanted to hear. For a week he had gone through in his mind, the names of artists and their hits, and he made a list of his favorite ones. What a difference a week made on his demeanor because of a song. But tragedy would hit him again and his family were concerned about his mental state after receiving some devastating news. I learned from one of the nurses that he was scheduled for surgery to remove his other leg within a couple of days.

    Revisiting him again after his surgery, it was clear this man no longer wanted to die. His family was surprised to see that he wasn't angry or bitter for losing his other leg and during his recovery he had made a longer list of songs for me to play. I grew up with a fondness for country music from the 1940s to the 1960s, so I had a catalogue of songs to draw from. During my time with him I spoke with some family members who told me that their father admired my talent and looked forward to seeing me every week. I have had feedback like this before from other family members throughout the years but this man's son said something I had never heard anyone say to me. Trying to keep his emotions in check his son said, "My father wanted to die. He just didn't want to live any more. He turned violently on my mother and sisters yelling he didn't want to see us anymore. But because of your weekly visits, your music and your genuine concern for him and the music he loves, you have saved my father's life. He is back to the father we once knew and still love." With misty eyes, he shook my hand and gave me a hug. I didn't know how to react after having never been told I saved a life.

This man had given his life a rebirth, perhaps by finding a reason for living in the lyrics of a country song and as a reminder of looking for everyday miracles one as simple as the dawn of a new day. He eventually left the hospital and we did see each other again in a senior living complex. The first time I played at the residence he now called home, I had learned that he referred me to the activity director and convinced her to get in touch with me to schedule a date for me to entertain the residents. As had happened in the hospital, when I was scheduled to play at the center, he had his list of songs he wanted to hear and I was happy to oblige. He has long since passed away but I still perform at that senior's complex. Now I am playing for his wife in another residence, and we always speak and remember him fondly for a few moments before I start to play. She always likes to hear the song "Lucille" by Kenny Rogers, which was one of her husband's favorite songs and artists. I can still see him in his wheelchair, a Canadian flag hanging from the back of his chair and his signature mark was his beer in the cup holder. He really loved his beer. Hank Williams Senior had a song out in 1950 – "There's a Tear in My Beer," and there was. Cheers my friend!

CHAPTER 23

I CAN'T BELIEVE YOU'RE STILL HERE

If something or an event takes you by surprise it can be looked upon as the greatest gift life can give you – to know that a small act in one's life can influence what can happen in the future. I've often wondered and asked myself why some people crossed my path at a certain point in my life.

In 2012, my wife and I were on our way to visit friends we met on a cruise who lived in Sarasota, Florida. We stopped at an outlet center in a local mall to purchase a suitcase for an upcoming fall trip. I had my wife speak to the salesperson because she knew not only what she was looking for but because she refuses to let me do the packing. She also knows that for a one-week cruise, I would pack clothing for a one-week cruise. My wife would pack clothes for a one-month cruise, along with the entire supply of beauty products, justifying the packing of both by a single phrase: "Just in case."

I was listening to their conversation and the salesperson's accent was familiar to me. I knew I had heard her accent before, but where? After a few moments, it dawned on me. After the salesperson was finished with my wife's acquisition, I said to her, "You're from Buffalo, New York!"

She said, "Yes!"

We had a long chat about Buffalo and about the amusement park in Crystal Beach, Ontario, which she frequented every summer when she lived in Buffalo. There was once a ferryboat, The SS Canadiana, an excursion steamer built in 1910, that took passengers on a return trip from Buffalo to Crystal Beach for the day. The ship was sold in 1956 and restoration efforts failed, the ship was scrapped in Port Colborne, Ontario, in 2004. I recognized her accent because of the number of people from Buffalo I had come to know very well who owned or rented a summer cottage at the beach. The salesperson remembered the park and the wax museum I managed during the summer of 1970. *Crystal Beach Amusement Park – The Good Old Days (1890/1989)*, a book by Erno Rossi, described the millions of people who frequented the park that was just as popular as the honorary wonder of the world, the Falls of Niagara, 31km away. I had two copies of the book and decided to send her my extra copy. Sometime later, I received her letter thanking me for the book and saying how much she enjoyed the reading. The surprising part was that in the book was a photograph of her and her ex-husband walking on the beach. In a way, the book brought back fond memories of a place she once called home. It was a chance meeting with an unexpected positive outcome for a former Buffalonian. This would not be my last surprise encounter of the kind.

 On my way to the office, I picked up a newspaper and for some reason I was compelled to check the obituary section before reading anything else. I recognized a woman I was singing for at the hospital. At lunchtime, I drove to the funeral home to pay my respects to her family. I met up with her daughter, who was pleased to see me and thanked me for the time I spent with her mother, and for bringing joy during her hospital stay. Years later, I had no idea what was coming my way and once again I would be taken by surprise and unprepared for an emotional encounter . . .

I was playing for a patient in a palliative care room and a woman in her early eighties wheeled herself up to the doorway. She kept staring at me and was misty-eyed as she smiled. After finishing my song, I walked over to her to say hello. I crouched down in front of her and she took my hand. Her face looked familiar but I couldn't seem to put a name to the face. She looked into my eyes then she said, "I can't believe you're still here!" Now my mind went into overdrive going through my memory bank, trying to remember who she was and where I'd seen her before. "You don't recognize me? You don't remember me?" I apologized to her for not remembering as I explained that during the many years I've spent as a volunteer at the hospital and outside care centers, it was very difficult for me to recall the many faces that I have met. When she revealed her identity, I was touched that this eighty-plus-year-old woman remembered me. I must have had an impact on her life for her to react in such an emotional way seeing me again.

It seems that many years ago I had sung for her mother on the same floor in the same hospital and that she thanked me once again for the joy I brought her mother and for taking the time to pay my respects to her when she passed away. The surprise here – it was her mother I read about, years before, in the obituary section of the newspaper I picked up on my way to the office. She asked if she could give me a hug. I put my guitar aside and gave her one. It was reciprocated with a gentle and loving pat on my back as she whispered, "I'm so happy to see you again."

Once again, I was taken by surprise by this emotional encounter. Now I was singing for her during her stay at the hospital and later at the senior residence she was transferred to. At the center, she always sat next to me and every so often she would tap me on the back to say she loved me as she did at the hospital. She once told me that my music made her want to live; she didn't want to die.

Before she passed, she asked that I sing at her funeral and I honored her request. History had repeated itself. I went to the same funeral home, where her mother once laid, to pay my respects to her family. Once again, I was thanked, this time by her daughter and granddaughter for the moments I spent with their mother and grandmother, reaffirming her affection for me. It was another chance meeting to prove without a doubt that someone's simple act of kindness could impact life for three generations.

CHAPTER 24

SHE REMEMBERED MY VOICE

I met Rita in the hospital's palliative care unit where her husband was recently transferred from another floor. He was on a priority list for a transfer to a senior's residence as soon as a room became available. After a few visits, Rita and I began to get acquainted. She spoke of her life with her husband, especially their travels to the various country music festivals in and around the area. They went all out, wearing cowboy boots, shirts and hats. Her husband would sometimes wear his dyed buckskin jacket which was elaborately detailed with a fringe on the pockets, collar and along the sleeves. The jackets were a staple of Western-wear, and a brief fad in the 1970s.

Her love for country music was undeniably true for she would list the artist's name and the songs that made him or her famous. Artists like Patsy Cline and George Jones, and Canada's own Hank Snow, whom I met several years before his passing. She was also a fan of current artists like Garth Brooks, Alan Jackson and Don Williams. It goes without saying I had no problems choosing any country song for their enjoyment. Rita was stout, soft spoken, gentle, and a grandmotherly type.

Unfortunately, her husband passed away before moving to a senior care center. During her husband's time at the hospital, the spouse of a friend of hers was also in the hospital but on a different floor. He too was on a priority list and was soon transferred to a residence where I still play on a regular basis. Thinking I would never see Rita again, in 2003 she surprised me when she attended an afternoon performance. From that moment, every time I played there, my oldest faithful fan would never miss a session to listen to me sing some of her favorite songs that she had enjoyed with her husband.

After a couple of years, she stopped coming to the residence. I was thinking that perhaps she was ill and would be back as soon as she was able to, or perhaps she went to join her late husband. If the latter was the case, I was just grateful for the privilege of having spent time with this *"grande dame."*

I can always expect to see new arrivals on the fourth floor either coming from another floor or from a family member whose parent or sibling need long- or short-term hospitalization. Such was the case of a sister who could no longer care for her brother at home. He was a tall, large man with a mental disability which I found strange because the floor was reserved mostly for palliative care patients. So, I was assuming that he would not pose any danger to the staff or myself if ever he reacted to something he did not approve of. I asked his sister if he liked music. She replied, "Oh yes very much so! He enjoys all kinds of music. I knew that music kept him calm and therefore I always had the radio on at home." I played him songs of the 1950s and 1960s and as his sister attested, he did stay calm and responded well to them. His sister was also aware of my weekly visits which comforted her knowing I would visit her brother again for as long as he was in the hospital. She also provided me with a list of artists and songs her brother reacted to and enjoyed hearing.

What I was unable to reveal to her was that one day I was playing in the kitchen for some of the patients when he came into the room. Something didn't seem right with him and he grew restless and inattentive. A nurse came into the kitchen to see if she could calm him down, but it was to no avail. He threw the first punch and missed her due to her quick response. I got up from my chair to remove my guitar around my neck and prepared to intervene if the situation intensified. The nurse was able to take control and led him out of the room. A similar situation occurred when I was with a patient when a woman with a more severe mental issue came in and tried in anger to grab my arm and guitar. My wife tried to ease her out of the room but she wanted no part of it and got very violent with my wife. A male nurse had to be called and they took the woman away to the kitchen not only for our safety but for hers as well. She was locked in the kitchen but was still able to see people walking by due to the half doors. Now it was on to the next room.

The woman in the neighboring room was also a new arrival and she was leaning to one side in her chair. I said hello to her and her roommate. I asked her if she was comfortable in her chair and if she wasn't I would get a nurse to help her straighten up. "No need," she said, "I'm fine!" So, I asked the new arrival what she would love to hear. Then I suddenly realized she was blind.

"What would you like for me to play madame?"

She said, "Play something like you did in the room next to me." A nurse told me she was ninety-three years old, and given that fact, I played something from the 1940s. Afterwards, she said that she and her husband loved country music, so I played Hank Williams' "Your Cheating

Heart" – a posthumous number-one hit from 1953, and she remembered her husband singing it. No sooner had I ended the song before she asked me for my name and when I told her, she said, "I know you, I remember you." I was stunned that this ninety-three-year-old woman immediately knew who I was. Her face looked familiar but it wouldn't come to me until she said that I had sung for her husband when he was here at the hospital years ago and that she had come to see me at a senior's care center, where her friend's husband lived. Then I knew who this lady was. This was where I first met Rita, in this hospital all those years ago. How moved was I to see Rita again. I held her hand and I didn't recognize this once heavy-set woman due to her extreme weight loss. She was blind and yet she remembered me by my voice and for something I had done for her husband nearly thirty years earlier.

On March 11th, 2020, tragedy struck. The Covid-19 pandemic was declared in Canada and with that hospital visits with Rita and others were brought to a temporary end. A year or so later, Rita's daughter called me to say that her mother was out of the hospital and living with her. It was something I was glad to hear but my heart was breaking for those patients at the hospital who were unable to see family members during that dreadful time in history. I decided, with her daughter's approval, to go to her house and play for Rita. I knew that I had to wear a mask to sing and I didn't mind it at all. Wearing one was protecting Rita, her daughter and myself. It was all worth it just to see the smile on Rita's face and the tears not of sadness but of happiness in her eyes. Though blind, I'm sure in her mind she was reliving the times with her husband at all those country music festivals.

The Healing Power of a Song

Rita is now ninety-seven years old and though much weaker she is still lucid and still very generous with her love and affection for me, as related to me by her daughter. I never thought for a moment that one day I would be playing for Rita in the same residence where she used to come to see and hear me play years before. She has never let her blindness bar her love for music or life and she tries her best to get out of bed whenever I'm playing at the residence so she can once again come to hear me play.

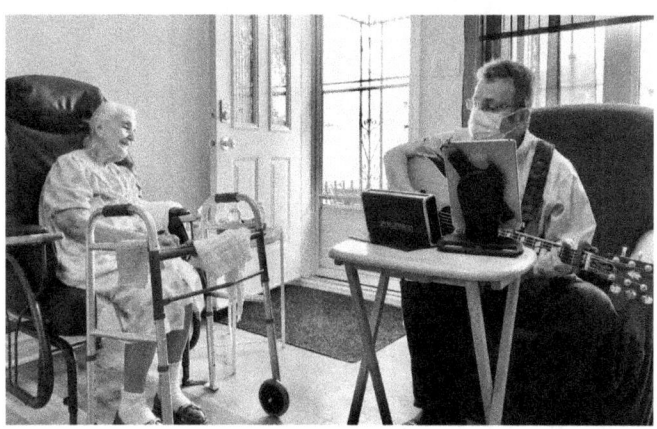

CHAPTER 25

MISS ANDREWS

When I met Miss Andrews, a petite woman with a charming smile, at the communal residence, it was obvious that she came from a well-to-do family. She was prim and proper, always behaving and never breaking the rules of etiquette. She was intelligent, cultivated and polite. This woman's qualities were put to the test one afternoon when I played for her and her fellow residents.

Knowing I was scheduled to be at the home on a particular day, she made sure she was wearing her finest dress, her hair was done, and she always had her pearl necklace on, along with fine jewelry for her ears and hands. She wore very little makeup with the help of a staff member, and she had the most captivating blue eyes. I told her that she must have broken many hearts in her day, and she put her hand on her chin and she simply smiled. She also knew and always looked forward to seeing me, as I would pay special attention to her as I did at every visit. I have always been drawn to the grandmotherly types, perhaps never having known my own maternal grandmother. I would kneel in front of her, singing one of her favorite songs. One of them was "Baby Face" by Al Jolson, who was one of the United States' most famous stars of the 1920s. He was also known as the "World's

Greatest Entertainer." She was an ardent fan of Jolson and followed his career until his death in 1950. I would look into Miss Andrews' eyes as I sang the lyrics, "Baby Face, you've got that cutest baby face," and there came that wonderful smile of hers. She also had this gleam of affection in her eyes. Perhaps in her mind, she was thinking of a suitor she became enamored with because of the way he might have sung the song to her as a young woman. Whatever the reason, she enjoyed every second of the two-minute-plus song.

Afterwards, I would ask her if she was having a good time and I would get a sweet "Oooh yes, of course!" Though the staff found the interaction with Miss Andrews adorable, I never knew that song had made me the culprit for instigating a verbal quarrel between Miss Andrews and some of the other female residents. I was also surprised about the altercation given Miss Andrews' rules of etiquette. No one told me how Miss Andrews reacted to the other women's comments. Someone may have said something she could not accept and voila, I guess everyone has their Achilles' heel.

It caused a great deal of excitement for the residents and a laugh for the staff who found it quite endearing that I could have stirred so much rivalry with a simple song. I didn't know how to react to something I had never experienced – initiating a "senior cat fight" with a song for a single woman – not even through all my rock n' roll years with the band. I had to accept the fact that my one and only "groupie" just happened to be a senior in her eighties.

Notwithstanding the position I put Miss Andrews in, she had nominated me for Volunteer of the Year, and during the evening ceremony, she sat next to me at the honors table. I told her that I was filled with gratitude for the nomination and I also apologized for the predicament

The Healing Power of a Song

I put her in that one afternoon and she just laughed it off. I knew deep down that was the only response I would get from this classy woman. I have never met anyone like Miss Andrews and believe I never will again. Before she passed away, I was told that she spoke often of me and how I had made Miss "Baby Face" Andrews feel special.

CHAPTER 26

OLIVER AND THE POLITICIAN

Before the arrival of winter's colder temperatures, shorter days and year-end holidays, Mother Nature applied her final brush of colors over the countryside. The arrival of fall was also a time for another political election campaign which was in full swing, and voting day was fast approaching. At this time, every politician would come calling, waving their political flag with a fraudulent smile of promises and hopes for the future. But there are some that will not capitulate to the politicians' proposed covenant within their constituency, and I witnessed it during my afternoon performance at a senior residence.

She came into the room with a politicians' self-important attitude and vain stance, looking for support for her party. Thus, begins Act 1: the con game, with the first resident being a woman in the early stage of Alzheimer's. The woman looked at the politician confused and unresponsive to the public servant's presence and what she was asking of her. The representative introduced herself, identified the party she was representing, shook her hand and asked the woman for her support. Then it was on to the next residents, who were very lucid, and the solicitation seemed to be going in her favor, she thought, as she made her way down the line.

Then she came across Oliver, the eldest resident and at the time still full of wit with his off-colored jokes and remarks he was famous for. Oliver loved women, but never in a disrespectful manner; he was a teaser. When the politician approached Oliver, sitting in his lazy boy chair, legs crossed with his face cupped in his right hand, she went through her babble – that's what it probably sounded like to Oliver. Then, with this devilish smirk he asked her, "Madame, do you have underwear on?" He had no interest in the politician nor her message, and I guess it was his way of asking if she had anything to hide. The staff, some of the residents and I laughed at his unexpected comment. That was Oliver! You never knew what he could come up with.

It was obvious that the politician did not find his remark amusing. With her bogus laugh, she quickly went on to the next person who was still chuckling over Oliver's off-the-cuff remark. She went on to lose the election.

Oliver's fondness for women and his sexual innuendos, which at times could make any religious leader blush, did not diminish even at the young age of ninety-five years old. One other thing about Oliver was that his faith was strong despite losing his wife, children, some grandchildren, his siblings and friends. He once told me, "We must accept what God sends us."

A woman who never knew much about Oliver once asked him about his life and if he had any children. She was unaware he had fathered twelve children and she was about to get a taste of his sense of humor. As he walked to the sunroom in a Charlie Chaplin fashion and before he sat down in his chair, she asked him if he could, would he be able to father another child, and of course he had a quick reply and said, "Let us give it a try."

When you're ninety-five years old, anything you say may be looked upon as "cute," which was the woman's reply to save face at his unexpected remark. Many seniors still enjoy their sexuality into their eighties and beyond, and Oliver often bragged that before his wife died, they had sex three times a week. Once, sitting in the sunroom, another couple was there when he once again boasted of his libido. The gentleman turned to his wife and said, "I can't wait to be his age." She gave him one nasty look and made it clear that his comment did not amuse her.

I had discovered that years before she passed, Oliver's wife said many times to family and friends that Oliver would die with exactly those sexual innuendos on his mind. On the day he passed away, a nurse I knew for many years described his last hours of his life. He was sitting up in his bed that morning waiting for his breakfast to arrive. When any female – whether it be a nurse or a staff member – came into his room, his mating ritual was put in full swing and he still wanted to give it a try with her. At three o'clock that afternoon he had laid down on his bed and a staff member came into his room raised his head to fluff up his pillow then covered him with a blanket, and before he closed his eyes, he winked at her, smiled and went into an eternal sleep. As predicted by his wife, he passed away with loving on his mind.

CHAPTER 27

ON THE ROAD AGAIN

In the fall of 1998, I was invited to attend a concert by a country music artist who was kicking off her European tour. Somehow, Rose heard of me and wanted to meet. We met in her dressing room at the concert hall and the first thing she asked me was if I had my guitar with me. It so happened I did because I was heading off to a friend's cottage a couple of hours away and what is an evening campfire without music under the stars? Then Rose said, "Great, you are going up on stage in a few minutes."

I wasn't expecting this at all. I thought it was only a meet and greet. What was I going to play once on stage without the security of my bandmates around me? I looked out at the crowd, at the faces of people who knew nothing about me. But I was determined to give it my best shot. After performing a couple of songs, I can't even remember what they were, I started to exit the stage with the applause of the crowd when I was approached by the organizers of a local country music festival. They booked me for the July 1999 and the July 2000 festivals. It was following my 2000 performance that a gentleman named Michael came to me and told how much he appreciated the show and my choice of songs. He asked if he could buy me a beer and for some reason I accepted this stranger's invitation.

So, we sat at a picnic table, beer in hand, and he began talking about his life. He said he had been in two wars and that he was once a semi-professional boxer and his Arnold Schwarzenegger-like physique and vice-grip handshake was proof enough to convince me. He was a man who loved to hunt and fish and it was apparent that he was also a huge fan of country music. About thirty minutes later it was time for me to be on the road for my next gig. I thanked him for the beer, wished him well and we parted ways.

A few years later, I was in an automotive store when I heard someone yell out my name. It was Michael. I must admit I was happy to see him again. Once more we sat together in a nearby restaurant having a cup of coffee and sharing our latest news. It didn't take me long to know that he also had a great sense of humor. At one point, he was being very serious, I thought, when he said, "You know my father was Russian and my mother was Russian," then he paused and said, "But I will take my time." I almost spit the coffee out of my mouth with laughter. That was the first time I took the bait like a fish on his reel but it wouldn't be the last time. Before leaving the restaurant, he invited me to visit him at his trailer he said was facing a lake and his boat which was moored to his private dock and that he would take me out fishing every day. He and his wife spent more than fifty summers there. She had died several years before but he was never alone. He had many friends at the trailer park who would visit with him. I had spent a few Sunday afternoons at the lake with him before I accepted his invitation to spend a weekend there. He had planned for me and my wife to stay in his friend's trailer. On the first morning, I woke up early and made my way to the dock. In the distance along the water's edge, the sun's golden rays were slowly rising above the tree line, awakening the senses, and I watched as the mist was slowly caressing

The Healing Power of a Song

the stillness of the lake and a loon's wail echoed across the air of a new day. This is when nature is at its best. It had been some time since I felt such internal peace.

At the end of the summer, it was time for Michael to lock up the trailer and prepare for the hunting season, only to find himself alone afterwards in his home. I visited Michael a few times at his residence and we would play music together. He had a honky-tonk piano and he played everything in the key of C major, which made it easy for me to accompany him on my guitar, even if the piano had one or more keys slightly detuned. Honky-tonk was a country style which began in the 1940s and was played by one of Michael's favorite country singers, Hank Williams Senior. He also loved Willie Nelson's song, "On the Road Again," which he played every time we got together and sometimes twice – once on the piano and once with his harmonica. There must have been a special attachment to the song related to his late wife. They must have done a great deal of traveling before settling down at the lake for the summer.

Before too long I started to see a change in Michael. His right hand was shaking, he would be out of breath after walking but a few steps, he seldom played his harmonica and he was losing weight. A social worker referred by a friend, suggested that Michael be sent to a senior residence where he would get the proper long-term care he would eventually need. He was getting weaker and could no longer live alone. On one of my visits with him at the residence, I brought my guitar to play some of his favorite songs. Of course, I had to play "On the Road Again." He asked me if I was still doing my volunteering at the hospital. Replying "Yes!" he said with his weakened voice, "Ah that's good!"

Michael was living in this very small room with a single bed, a single chair and a dresser with a single picture on it of him and his late wife. Often, he would tell me how much he loved and missed her as he was trying to hide the tears from his eyes. He was looking forward to seeing her again so that he could give her a hug and a great big kiss. I never knew his age and I was surprised to learn that he was ninety years old. He was in such great shape, always active, which hid his real age.

The last time I saw him, this man who was once strong as an ox, was now feeble, bent over in his chair with his body consumed with cancer. Was it providence that brought us together in 2000, filling a void in each other's lives? Was it really meant to be? I could not have believed that knowing this man for such a short time, I would be spending a great deal of time with him, for the remainder of his life, sharing music that he loved and listening to the stories he had to tell. In the middle of one of his stories, Michael paused and asked for a glass of water. He was gone before he was able to drink it. He was on the road again, on heaven's highway, heading to his final destination where I am sure his wife was waiting.

I have been volunteering for over fifteen years, playing at churches, hospitals, and senior residences when I met Michael. This led to requests for me to play at numerous funeral services. I was dealing with death so much at one point that it was starting to wear on me emotionally. It's one thing to play and sing at funerals for families who have lost a loved one, but I was also losing friends. It nearly caused me to stop volunteering.

Meeting Michael was meant to be...it was fate. It is said what goes around comes around. I was not giving something to Michael during his final days, I was unknowingly the recipient. Michael left me a gift when he invited me to stay that one weekend at his trailer. It was a gift of finding peace I so longed for by a tranquil lake with the soothing tremolo of a loon giving me the strength to carry on with my volunteer work.

CHAPTER 28

WORKPLACE CHARITABLE CAMPAIGN

From 1994 to 1999 I was involved with my department's Workplace Charitable Campaign. During my last year with the department, I orchestrated a ninety-minute show for the opening ceremonies for three fundraising events. I solicited a couple of musicians – my childhood friend and bandmate John was on drums and a keyboard player – and we rehearsed a setlist not only for the newly formed trio's performance, but as a backup band for singers invited to showcase their talents for a good cause. One of the events took place in the atrium of my building. There was an oval stage on the lower level, surrounded by a food market, post office, restaurant and bookstore. As the group was setting up the sound system, microphone, drums, keyboard and guitar pedals, people were curious about the event being held in the center court. Some wondered if a politician would be giving a speech, given the proximity to the seat of the federal government. When they learned that we were putting on a show to raise funds for our Workplace Charitable Campaign, they decided to stay for the recital.

Before our live performance, a sound check was conducted to ensure that the sound facing the audience and the sound on stage which is heard through our on-stage monitors was clear and set to the proper volume and frequencies. Then the trio did a couple of warm-up numbers which attracted more spectators.

With all the band members in place and before the first chord of the introductory song was played, I was able to observe the number of spectators increasing around the three floors above the center of the atrium and in front of the stage. Now it was time to raise the imaginary curtain, and in the words of Ed Sullivan, I said, "We have a really big shoe" for you this afternoon. About thirty minutes into the program the audience was made aware of the main reason for putting on the show.

After introducing my fellow performers, some of my colleagues headed into the crowd; some were dancing and putting on a show of their own and collecting donations in the process. Moving right along, we had one of our guest singers come up to the microphone to do her number. This gave me an opportunity to look at the crowd to gauge their reaction to the show and the music. It was then I noticed an elderly woman sitting alone on a bench. She had her dark winter coat on with a dark scarf hanging around her neck and her purse was by her side. She waved over one of my colleagues and the two had a short chat.

After a couple of encores, the show was over and my colleague who chatted with the woman told me that this lady sitting on the bench wanted to see me and to bring my guitar. With the spectators leaving, I exited the stage with my guitar in hand and made my way towards the bench where this small woman was waiting. I introduced myself and I sat next to her. She gave us high praise for the show and the music selection. Then she began by talking about her late husband who passed away a couple of months before. Now I understood why she was all dressed in black. I asked her the reason for wanting to see me. Then she said, "If you can play my special request I will donate to the cause."

I took her hand and I told her if I knew the song I would be happy to play it for her, whether she donated or not. She had requested, "The French Song" (Quand le soleil dit bonjour aux montagnes), a 1965 hit made famous by Lucille Starr. She said her husband was a Francophone and he sang the song often to her. She went on to say that after having had the song sung to her many times over the years, she paused and laughed a bit, it had allowed her to learn some French words. Her comment brought back a memory of the time Oliver, who never missed a cue to exude his wit, met the politician. He once said that he himself wanted to learn the English language and he had spent three nights with an English woman but didn't learn a thing.

I knew the song this woman asked for and after playing it she made a very generous donation, more than anyone expected from a woman who appreciated this fond memory of the past evoked by a single song. With misty eyes, she gave this wonderful tender embrace, kissed me on the cheek, and whispered softly in my ear, "Thank you, merçi et bonne journée!" Once again, a song had the power to touch a soul, to be a source of solace for a woman who had recently lost her husband. She slowly walked and disappeared, like the character Chance, played by Peter Sellers in his last movie, *Being There.* To this day I cherish a wonderful photograph taken of us sitting on that bench.

CHAPTER 29

HISTORY SET TO MUSIC

On November 11th, 1998, Remembrance Day, I had been asked to play at a public school for students in grades four through eight. Playing for seniors is one thing but trying to entertain students from the ages of nine to fourteen would prove to be challenging. My repertoire was not as extensive back then as it is today, so finding songs to amuse this crowd would require some sort of inspiration. There weren't many songs in my repertoire that didn't have a theme of bad love, infidelity, revenge or spending all night at a bar. The only song I remember at that time I had was "Puff the Magic Dragon" by Peter Paul and Mary, released in 1963, which I knew deep down inside wouldn't go over well, especially with the older students. Then I had an epiphany! What better way to learn about history this Remembrance Day, than with a short background of a historical event followed by a song written about it. I had a thirty-minute show to put on and found all that I needed for a successful performance.

    I was backstage watching the students coming into the gymnasium and I was more frightened of going out on stage and facing them than I was when asked, just a month or so before, to go on another stage within minutes, cold and unprepared.

The teachers and students had taken their seats and I was reviewing my quick setlist and going through the introduction for each song in my mind. When the school principal came on stage, the gymnasium became suddenly quiet. I was introduced and walked on stage to applause. Standing there, I took a few seconds to peruse the crowd. The difference between this group and the ones I was used to was that I would have to work hard to avoid the yawning, and I may have to resort to my limited comical skill.

I started my show by asking those who love horses to raise their hand. The response was good and so my first song was about a horse named Comanche. I now had their attention and went on to say that Comanche was with Lieutenant Colonel George Armstrong Custer at the Battle of the Little Bighorn. After a short summary of the battle, they learned that Comanche was badly wounded but managed to get back to the fort and was nursed back to health. That happy ending received an applause. As I sang the song, I could see they hung on to every lyric. Watching their faces I could also see they were captivated by Comanche's story – that he fought hard, that he was a good soldier, and that he was a symbol of bravery. Before playing my next piece of history between the British and the Americans, I gave the students an abridged version of the Battle of New Orleans, which was fought on January 8th, 1815, and the absurdity was that the war of 1812 was officially over on December 24th, 1814. I also sang "North to Alaska," about the Klondike Gold Rush of 1896 where an estimated 100,000 people tried to reach the goldfields but there were around 30,000 – 40,000 who eventually made it. The final historical event, the sinking of the Bismarck ("Sink the Bismarck"), took place during the Second World War. I revealed to my history class that in 1941 the

The Healing Power of a Song

Germans had a super-battleship named the Bismarck, which was the fastest ship ever to sail the sea. But when I described The Bismarck as having the most powerful guns on its deck and its shells were bigger and more powerful than any of the cannonballs used in the Battle of New Orleans, I got a huge "Wow!" The four historical songs I performed were recorded by Johnny Horton, an American Country musician who died on November 5th, 1960 at the age of 35, in an automobile accident. He may have been on stage with me on that November day. His contribution to some historical events got me out of what could have been a very embarrassing performance.

For my final number, I chose the Italian song that I played for a young, handicapped boy in a senior residence that requires the participants to raise their arm, left or right and say "Hey!" after the lyric "Whatsa matter you!" The students really participated along with the teachers and it was a good time for all.

The history lesson over, I made my way off stage and for a few minutes I chatted with some of the students before returning to their classroom. I was surprised that a couple of them thanked me for the history lessons, adding they had learned something. As some of them made their way out of the gymnasium a few of them turned around raised their arms and said "Hey!" Receiving feedback in this manner made volunteering my time with them more gratifying and a rewarding experience.

Looking back, perhaps I would have enjoyed being a history teacher, and I know my high school history teacher would have been proud of the lessons I gave those students that day, especially using the unique method of song lyrics of an historical event as an educational tool.

CHAPTER 30

HOW DID SHE KNOW

I have met hundreds of people over the years. Some were sad, some were funny, some were just mean and miserable, some were violent and some were just fed up with life. I walked into this hospital room and I came face to face with a person with a sort of demonic look in her eyes and if looks could kill, well, I would have been one of her victims. She was obviously very angry about something. Within a few moments of letting her vent her frustration, I quickly learned that it wasn't something that angered her but someone – it was her husband. She was convinced he betrayed her. It seems that she had been in a coma for a few weeks and when she awoke, she expected her husband to be by her side. He had promised her that he would never leave her, that he would always be there to take care of her, and when the time came to part, that he would leave after her so that she would not be left alone. During her state of unconsciousness, her husband had passed away and had already been laid to rest.

With no children and now no husband to care for her, she took out her anger on everything and everyone. I was told that she would yell at the nurses, toss her meals on the floor and use profanity to amplify her anger. I never knew the whole story until I walked into her room. When I looked into this woman's eyes I could see and feel that she didn't want me anywhere near her. She did not waste any time in bringing down the hammer of her anger on me. I calmly conveyed to her that I was sorry for her loss, gave her my sincere condolences and promised her that I would see her next time I was in the hospital. My only regret was that I had left the other woman in the room deprived of a bit of joy. I had to be realistic, that it was not the appropriate time for music or any type of interaction. I also knew that I was the elephant in the room and it was time for me to continue to the sanctuary of the next room.

My second visit with her was a bit more pleasant, though she was still angry. I said hello and asked her "How are you today? If you do not want any music we can just talk if you wish." She was still hanging on to her resentment towards her husband and I attempted to digress from the subject matter by again offering to play something she would like to hear or we simply just talk. I told her that it would be good for her roommate as well to hear a song as she was deprived the last time I was in the room. After a few moments, she agreed to one song and said adamantly, "That's all . . . just one song for her!"

Not willing to push my luck, after the song ended, I said that I would certainly see her again next week. Leaving the room, I could see that she was now more approachable and I was convinced that my third visit with her would be slightly more enjoyable.

When I arrived at the hospital for my third visit with her, I was wondering if she would still be there as I reflected on the last time I saw her. I made my way to her room and it was plain to see that there was a noticeable change in her demeanor. Her eyes were more welcoming and we chatted a bit before asking her if she would like to hear a song – one that she would prefer to hear; something that may bring back a pleasant memory of better days with her husband.

I only played one song, "I'll Never Find Another You," a 1964 hit by The Seekers. I thought if she would only listen closely to the lyrics, it would remind her of the wonderful life she had with her husband.

Once it was over, I calmly asked her if she would like to hear another selection. I was sure she would reject the suggestion outright as she did on my second visit with her. We chatted a bit more and to my disbelief she wanted to hear "Tennessee Waltz," a song made famous in 1956, by Patti Page. Perhaps the first song did instill in her a nostalgic moment in her life with her spouse, for as soon as I completed the song this woman took me by surprise when she said firmly to me, "If you have something to do, do it now." You would think that saying it once the way she did was enough, but no, she said it again, raising her voice and pointing her finger at me; "If you have something to do, do it now."

Did the two songs I played trigger something in her? I didn't know what to make of this revelation, nor what the meaning behind it was. What kind of premonition did she have about my future? I must admit I did not leave the hospital undaunted by her remark.

For several months, my wife and I were contemplating a long trip and we just could not seem to agree on whether we should go or stay home. Our main issue was not the cost of the trip, but the length of time and distance away from home. Our procrastination came to an end after I told my wife what this woman who was once filled with anger said to me. My wife was also taken aback by her remark and concerned about it as well. It had to be now or never, so we booked the trip. This woman gave me a sign which

I didn't ignore, a message that your life can change in an instant, like hers, without warning.

It was on this trip we met our traveling friends with whom for more than a decade we have traveled the world; something that never would have happened had it not been for that once-livid woman I met so many years ago.

Many times, I have asked myself this question: how did she know? How did she know about our procrastination about a trip – something I had never ever mentioned to her during our brief conversations? Once again it was something that could not be explained. No matter the answer, I'm so grateful to a woman whose life was changed by her personal grief and in turn changed my life because of a simple act of kindness, a sympathetic ear and perhaps a song of healing.

CHAPTER 31

MORE THAN A CENTURY

Sometimes it can be difficult not to let your emotions or feelings get the best of you when meeting the elderly, the terminally ill or the physically challenged. There may be times when the scenes of the deteriorating condition of a patient can be overwhelming. I admit when I signed up to be a volunteer at hospitals and senior homes, I knew that it wasn't going to be easy. I was afraid to fail in bringing some sort of solace to people I had never met.

In time, I made it a point not to look at the illness and the reason why they were hospitalized. My objective was to make them smile or laugh or sing and dance if they could. For the short time I'm in a room, I want the patients to enjoy the moment, to feel good and to have them say their spirits were raised and that they needed something like music that day and looking forward to another visit.

I remember a dark and dreary rainy April day with no break in sight. As I look back now, this was probably a sign of what was in store for me as I walked into the center.

At the entrance of a woman's room, the first thing I saw on the wall in front of me was a large single photograph of her standing next to an unidentified young man wearing a cowboy hat. She doesn't notice me right away. Quietly, she listens to a random show playing on her television. She is sitting in her lazy boy chair, weighing barely eighty pounds, with a blanket covering her frail body and a large picture of Jesus with a lamb around His neck and with His finger pointing up hanging on the wall behind her. She can no longer see out of her left eye and her right eye is slightly opened. Her hair is all but gone. Her face and hands are covered in various sizes of deep brown age spots. The skin on her arms is paper thin, leaving several bruises like ecchymosis on them. She has a swan-neck deformity of her fingers, indicating a severe case of rheumatoid arthritis. She is also suffering from edema, affecting her feet and ankles, caused by her prolonged sitting. There isn't a single indication, such as photographs, of family members still living on the walls or her dresser. Her voice is raspy and her speech is obviously subsiding, which makes it difficult to understand her. However, I was able to ascertain that she once loved and now misses dancing by her constant effort to move her legs as the music enters her consciousness. She undoubtedly has a great love of music by her long, deep, audible breath expressing her approval of the music with a "yes!"

After a short and difficult conversation with this lady, my first impression was that this remarkable woman seemed to accept the reality of her condition and still embraced life, this woman of a hundred and one years old, with a kindhearted smile. It was a good indication that the music I played for her was making her feel good and her smile lit up her face with a genuine warmth and joy to every song she knew.

At one point, it was clear to me that anything I played took her back to a point in time. While she was still embracing life, it was obvious, though she would never admit it, that she was suffering and hoping in silence for the day she would be led by a beaconing bright light to heaven's gate, perhaps meeting up with all those she loved who had gone before her. Trying to keep my emotions and feelings within my being in her presence, seeing her in the physical state she was in, had me asking myself where people like her find the courage and the strength to endure life's trials and tribulations that test their resilience, strength, and character. Before leaving, she requested the gospel song, "I'll Fly Away." Though she could not sing it out loud, she did so in her mind because she remembered St Augustine saying, "He who sings prays twice." Afterwards, there was this haze of peace and tranquility in the room as she fell asleep in her chair.

CHAPTER 32

THE ESSAY

Volunteering your time at a hospital, a senior care center, and raising funds for charitable organizations at your church or anywhere there is a need for your talent or services will enrich your life. Dedicating your time as a volunteer reflects who you are as an individual and the rewards are priceless.

With the many accolades, thanks and appreciation I have received over the years, it was a primary school project in 1988, that made me aware of what kind of an impact my involvement in the community can have on others, especially one seven-year-old student.

I received a phone call from the child's parents wanting me to attend a ceremony at his primary school and how it would be very important to their son if I could be there. The students would be presenting their essays on the person they had high praise for. I was totally surprised and at a loss for words in being the subject of their son's essay.

Of all the relatives he loved, like his uncle, grandfather, and even his father, he chose me as a role model he admired most. For days, I kept wondering why he would choose me as his school project. I would see the young boy at mass and I spoke very little to him until he decided to get closer to me. But his heartfelt testimonial would answer my questions. He wrote: "I would like to tell you about a very nice person who has become a good friend for me. Henri is his name. He is the musician of my community's church. At the beginning, when he started playing the guitar in church, I sat near my parents. Then, I moved closer to him to look at him better and listen to him. I admired his talent and his music. With that, quite simply, we got to know each other. The day he asked me to hold his guitar, I was excited. My heart was pounding in my stomach. My parents were happy for me. Henri has a beautiful voice and he invites everyone to accompany him. He even asked me to sing at the microphone. He encourages me to faithfully practice my piano, so that we can one day play together. At Christmas mass, he had wrapped a small gift for me. He wanted to tell me he loved me. Between you and me, he is much more than a friend: he is a great example of sharing and friendship. I admire him a lot and I want to be like him."

After the ceremony, this remarkable young man sat behind a piano and played for me. His father had taken a photograph of the two of us at the piano which hangs proudly on my wall in my office. When I first read Leo Buscaglia's quote about giving of oneself, I never thought that one day I would impact the life of a child by a simple act of kindness. To have received love and admiration from this young lad was a powerful and priceless gift.

CHAPTER 33

KINDRED SPIRITS

Seventeen years ago, I had the great fortune of meeting my wife Carole-Anne as a volunteer providing music for a touring stage troop in which she was part of the cast.

Recognizing each other as kindred spirits, within a few months of our relationship, she got on board as a volunteer at the hospital. She has not only changed my personal life but has impacted my volunteer work at the hospital and senior residences. She is empathic, compassionate and deeply dedicated to the mission. She is stout of heart. Very few have this beautiful ability to change other people's lives. She treats everyone with love and respect which is reciprocated tenfold. She is simply a natural that possesses an inner beauty of elegance, refinement and a touch of quirkiness. Volunteerism does have its rewards and having Carole-Anne in my life is proof. We share the same values and goals thus creating a strong relationship between ourselves and the community we serve. I am very proud of her and grateful for her contribution to this literary endeavor.

Carole-Anne, you and I are like music and love, we are natural allies.

CHAPTER 34

THE HEALING POWER OF A SONG

I am blessed to have been handed down a talent to play the guitar, an instrument once played by my father Angelo, a man I never knew. An instrument that introduced me to several people who for some have become very close friends or family. This old guitar has been part of my fabric from the age of thirteen, when I was influenced by seeing The Beatles one night in 1964 on that small black and white television set sitting on a shelf. For me, these four young mop-topped lads from Liverpool, England, were bigger than life.

    This old rosewood guitar has given meaning to my life and the opportunity to reach my initial and ongoing goal of improving life in my community. The songs played on this old guitar have opened a world of artistic beauty through the melodic colorful sounds of its strings combined with lyrics that convey messages of hope and healing to the listeners. The songs played on this old guitar have shared the joy, the pain, the laughter and the final chapters of many lives. Parents, whether biological or not, can be a disappointment to their children, and the songs played on this old guitar comforted me through times of mental and physical abuse at the hands of an intemperate stepfather. The songs played on this old guitar helped me to cope with a woman who failed to come to the defense of her firstborn from a stepfather who never accepted a child she had before they married. A woman who refused to be called ma or mom, and who turned siblings against one another because of her lies and deception.

Despite it all, the songs played on this guitar gave me the will and the strength to carry on and not succumb to an unhappy pass by turning to drugs or alcohol, but to use the pass to solidify my resolve in determining my own future and to follow my own compass. The songs played on this guitar have shown me that I can be sensitive and compassionate towards others through the power of strong lyrics I can also relate to.

During those long nights spent practicing chords, learning songs and achieving something despite my personal trials and tribulations, the songs played on this guitar have taught me about perseverance, to never give up or give in, giving me solace when I really need it most, and thus starting my own healing process. The songs played on this guitar helped me to deal with the personal loss of a close family member, a friend, and all those who came afterwards. The songs played on this guitar have allowed me to share my love of music with others and it has also revealed the reality that one day I may no longer be able to sing or play this instrument or no longer see it as a source of joy but of pain. I pray that I will pass away peacefully in my sleep before that happens. For the present, until I am called back home, I will continue my mission I started some four decades ago for as long as I have my health.

Someone once said that we live twice – once when we are born, and again in the stories we leave behind. I hope that my stories will inspire readers to get involved in their communities. They will never regret being a volunteer;

they may, however, regret not starting sooner, but again, it's never too late. Committing to the service of others is a reminder that I am part of something greater than myself and to never underestimate the healing power of a song. Leo Buscaglia wrote: "Your talent is God's gift to you; what you do with it is your gift to God." I pray that God has accepted my gift in return for the one He gave to me, and that I have used it well for the betterment of the lives of His children. If not, He had thirty days to return the gift. I'm sure God appreciates the levity, as it comes from another gift he gave me, that of a good sense of humor. I can't think of a better way to end this literary endeavor!

The End

www.ingramcontent.com/pod-product-compliance
Lightning Source LLC
LaVergne TN
LVHW011949070526
838202LV00054B/4866